The River of Life

The River of Life

Changing Ecosystems of the Mekong Region

YOS SANTASOMBAT

MEKONG PRESS

Mekong Press was initiated in 2005 by Silkworm Books with the financial support of the Rockefeller Foundation. In 2007, the Mekong Press Foundation was registered as a nonprofit organization to encourage and support the work of local scholars, writers, and publishing professionals in Cambodia, Laos, Vietnam, and the other countries in the Greater Mekong Subregion. Books published by Mekong Press (www.mekongpress. com) are marketed and distributed internationally. Mekong Press also holds seminars and training workshops on different aspects of book publishing, and helps find ways to overcome some of the huge challenges faced by small book publishers in the region.

ISBN: 978-616-90053-2-2

Published in 2011 by
Mekong Press
6 Sukkasem Road, T. Suthep
Chiang Mai 50200 Thailand
info@mekongpress.com
http://www.mekongpress.com

Photographs by Wichean Unprasert, Paiboon Hengsuwan, Satien Chunta and Tim Santasombat

Typeset in Scala 10 pt. by Silk Type
Printed and bound in China

5 4 3 2 1

Contents

Foreword

Anthropologist Yos Santasombat has again produced a book that deserves the full attention of those interested in resource management and development, and especially, of those concerned with the future of the Mekong River and its riparian communities. One of the world's major rivers, the Mekong embodies the spirit of mainland Southeast Asia. From the mountains of Tibet to the South China Sea, its waters bind together six countries: China, Burma, Thailand, Laos, Cambodia, and Vietnam. Its magnificence inspires respect and awe, and its waters and fisheries are a source of livelihood for millions of people.

As the book tells it, the six riparian countries joined hands in the early 1990s to promote growth by establishing the Greater Mekong Subregion (GMS) integrated economic area, under the encouragement of the Asian Development Bank and other international donors. The proposed market- and infrastructure-oriented model of regional integration aims to facilitate the movement of goods and investments, and maximize the use of natural resources in an environmentally sound and socially equitable manner in order to boost economic growth and lift out of poverty the estimated 30 percent of the region's 310 million people still lacking basic standards of living.

In this context, the Mekong's waters provide a test case to assess whether integration is indeed occurring as envisioned. Examining the lives and livelihoods of riparian communities in Yunnan, Laos, and Thailand, the book questions whether the benefits and costs of development are indeed equally shared across countries and groups, and whether economic growth has not occurred to the detriment of the region's social and environmental habitat. The vivid descriptions of riparian communities struggling to adapt to rapidly changing circumstances make clear that the promised gains of regional integration have been elusive to some of the GMS people.

For the studied communities, ongoing economic and social transformations are resulting in increased vulnerability, cultural fragmentation, and environmental degradation. As transnational processes evolve, they are losing control over land, water, and forest resources; they are not sharing in the benefits; and are becoming disproportionately burdened with the social and environmental impacts. This is occurring because their needs and priorities are not consistent with those of the more powerful stakeholders operating at the national and regional levels. As mentioned in the book, regional interest in hydroelectric dams as a source of energy and foreign exchange conflicts with riparian communities' interest in biodiversity conservation and preservation of fishing livelihoods.

While depicting a stark future for less advantaged Mekong communities, the book still gives reason to hope by pointing out that these communities have the capacity to react. Their local knowledge is continuously transformed into adaptive responses that allow them to cope with evolving historical realities. For instance, in response to erratic fluctuation of water levels, many local communities have devised conservation measures to regulate the timing and extent of fishing. It is the author's belief that if the value of this knowledge is recognized, and communities are included in regional and national planning, a sounder natural resource management system can be fostered. Consequently, the book advocates the incorporation of bottom-up planning processes in the development of the GMS. Considering the unequal power structure within and across countries, however, communities may not be able to spur a more inclusive approach on their own. Here is where the book emphasizes that the formation of transnational civil society alliances between local groups and regional and international organizations is crucial to more balanced development in the GMS.

The book's call for involving communities as partners in development should indeed be seriously considered by policy makers and regional planners. As the future of the Mekong River is more than ever linked to the future of the region, the people who live along its waters should have a central role in envisioning adequate development models and in identifying solutions to what have now become their problems. Only then will the unprecedented expression of transnational unity benefit those most directly affected by the river transformations.

May the book be widely read and its holistic perspective of development well-received for the Mekong to continue to flow and for regional development to become sustainable.

Dr. Rosalia Sciortino
Associate Professor
Institute of Population and Social Research
Mahidol University

Preface

Natural resources in the Mekong Basin and diverse systems of ecological knowledge and management are being dangerously threatened by megaprojects designed to exploit the basin's natural wealth for corporate profits and national economic development. A combination of state and private sector investments in hydroelectric dams, a navigational project, highways, tree plantations, mining, and other infrastructural projects are transforming the Mekong and its tributaries along with the region's land and forests—the essence of local livelihood security—into expendable resources for commercial investment and exploitation. Despite promises of shared benefits to wider populations in the region, megaprojects have in fact degraded natural resources and impoverished many local communities.

This book describes the transnational enclosure of the Basin's natural resources in the name of regional and national development. It tells how megaprojects have adversely affected marginal communities in Yunnan, Laos, and northern Thailand, whose resource bases have been encroached upon, expropriated, and degraded. This book also reflects on efforts made by local communities in the Mekong Basin to build and extend a version of environmental experiments and social advocacy that links participation, social justice, and nature management agendas under the rubric of local networks of resource management.

The proposal for local networks of resource management is based on several premises: that local communities have a greater interest in the sustainable management of natural resources than does the state and the private sector; that local groups are more knowledgeable when it comes to the intricacies of ecological systems and processes; and that local communities are more effective in resource management using traditional and hybrid forms of environmental conservation practices. In describing the link between transnational enclosure and environmental degradation in the Mekong region, this book seeks to bring about a rethinking of how the goals of sustainable development and viable resource management can be linked to the search for participation and inclusion of marginal communities, whose members have long been the stewards of the Mekong. Ultimately, this book discusses the role of transnational civil society, which could serve as a forum where the voices of all stakeholders in the Mekong basin can be heard, and a negotiated space of good governance and participation in the true sense of the comanagement of natural resources between local and national agencies can be strengthened.

A chance meeting with local teachers and villagers in Chiang Khong at the turn of the millennium provided an impetus for me to search for a new project about local people and their struggles. Some months later, a Lue woman I met in Luang Prabang inspired this research. It was not the sad face of the woman who was hitching a ride from her village to the city to visit her husband that touched me. It was not even the baby loosely strapped on her back. It was her story, a story of a fisher family forced to look for a new livelihood in the urban area, a story that since then I have heard hundreds of times from many riparian villages in Laos and Thailand.

This project started in early 2004 but was rudely disrupted for more than a year by prolonged affliction. In January 2005, three weeks after the Tsunami wreaked havoc in Southeast Asia, I had atrial fibrillation which caused an embolism/embolic stroke and was hospitalized for four weeks. I ended up spending the next year at home trying to recuperate and partially regain my strength through physical therapy. In the most difficult situation, however, there were rays of hope and a constant stream of support from friends and colleagues, research assistants, and graduate students. I wish to express my deepest appreciation to Lung Saw, Khamsing, Saeng and many other fisher folk who taught me and my associates many invaluable lessons from the grassroots. I wish to thank our Chinese colleagues, Dr. Yu Xiaogang and Ms. Yunfeng Yang at Green Watershed for their contribution and assistance with field research in Sipsong Panna, Yunnan. Mr. Sianouvong Savathvong and Mr. Boonpeng Pengchan at Luang Prabang's Provincial Forestry Office served as primary researchers in various riparian communities in Laos. I also wish to thank my colleagues and graduate students, especially Wichean Unprasert, Paiboon Hengsuwan, and Satien Chunta, three researchers who have been an integral part of this research endeavor from its inception. My sincere thanks also to Aranya Siriphol and Palaiwan Srisaringkarn for a constant stream of support and assistance.

The research in Yunnan, Luang Prabang, and northern Thailand was conducted under the auspices of the Rockefeller Foundation and Thailand's Biodiversity Research and Training Program (BRT). I am extremely appreciative of this support. I would like to express my gratitude to Professor Visuth Baimai, Director of BRT for his continuing support and to Dr. Rosalia Sciortino, former Regional Representative for Southeast Asia at the Rockefeller Foundation, for her support and especially for her kind foreword to this book. I would like to thank Ms. Sabrina Gyorvary for editing the first draft of the manuscript. I am most appreciative of Khun Trasvin Jittidecharak and Ms. Susan Offner as well as all the staff at Mekong Press for their kind editing and preparation of the manuscript. Finally, my wife and children always help define new perspectives on life and living that make the difficulties of writing seem much more bearable and at times enjoyable.

PART I
CONCEPTS AND RATIONALE

Introduction

The great Mekong River is the tenth largest river in the world and one of the most important rivers in Asia. The Mekong has its origins in the Tibetan plateau. Its first 2,000 kilometers, the Upper Mekong Basin, with a watershed of approximately 190,000 square kilometers flows 2,400 kilometers through China's Yunnan Province. The Mekong then flows on to five other countries downstream before entering into the South China Sea through the "Nine Dragons," the huge delta in southern Vietnam. The 600,000 square kilometers of watershed draining into the Mekong from these countries is known as the Lower Mekong Basin.

Covering over 2.3 million square kilometers, the Mekong Basin encompasses Yunnan Province in China, Laos, Burma, Thailand, Cambodia, and Vietnam, and is home to over 240 million people and more than 100 different ethnic groups. It is rich in both biological and cultural diversity. Areas where the Mekong joins with several tributaries in these countries are characterized by diverse ecosystems and forest types, seasonal fluctuation of environmental conditions, and a rich variety of fish. Local communities throughout the Mekong Basin have learned how to live with these diverse ecosystems; they have developed sophisticated knowledge regarding environmental management, fish ecology, fishing gear, fishing techniques, and rules and ritual practices to manage their common property. This local knowledge has been passed down from generation to generation and incorporated into the cultures and societies of the people who live by the Mekong.

During the wet season, flood water inundates river basins and migratory fish enter tributary rivers for spawning. Flooded river basins provide spawning grounds for migratory fish species. The livelihood of local peoples in these watershed areas has depended upon migratory fish and a fluctuating riparian environment for centuries. In accordance with seasonal fish migration behavior, local people have exploited aquatic resources using various techniques and fishing gear at different places in varying ecosystems. Thousands of reservoirs and ponds along the Mekong's tributaries provide not only good fishing grounds for local fishing villages, as well as inland and upland communities, but also important spawning and nursery grounds for many fish species.

Over the past decade, however, the Mekong Basin has undergone rapid socioeconomic, cultural, and political change. Guided by a growth-oriented economic development model, increasing transnational coop-eration in infrastructural development, and freer cross-border flows of people and commercial goods, is posing serious challenges to existing cultures, subsistence practices, and local knowledge. Current patterns of resource use and development also have varying impacts on different groups. Poor and marginal communities who depend upon the forests, rivers, and other natural resources for their subsistence needs find it increasingly difficult to cope with the winds of change as megaprojects such as the construction of roads and hydroelectric dams lead to forest degradation, soil erosion, and other environmental problems. Increasing poverty and widening income gaps, health issues, socioeconomic problems, and the trafficking of women and children from marginal groups have accompanied subregional growth and development.

This book aims at developing a better understanding of transnational megaprojects, especially the construction of hydropower dams on the Mekong, and their impact on changing ecosystems and the lives and livelihoods of marginal communities in the Lower Mekong Basin. It examines how changing ecosystems have impacted both fish ecology and local cultures and economies. The study provides a socioeconomic analysis of aquatic and forest products in relation to the economies and cultures of marginal communities, and identifies changes in lifestyles, local knowledge, and ritual practices as adaptive responses of these marginal communities to change. The focus is on four types of marginal communities along the Mekong and its tributaries, its wetland areas and upland ethnic communities in northern Thailand, northern Laos, and southern China.

Fishing communities along the Mekong River include local communities in Chiang Saen and Chiang Khong in Chiang Rai Province, northern Thailand, Luang Prabang Province in Laos, and Sipsong Panna in Southern China. Specific locations include Ban Hat Khrai, Chiang Khong and Ban Huai Kiang, Chiang Saen in Thailand; Ban Huai Xai, in Bo Kaew Province in Laos; and Manfeilong, Manfadai, and Manlong in Muang Han, Chiang Rung in Yunnan.

Communities in areas where the Mekong joins with tributaries include those of the Ing River in northern Thailand, the Nam Khan, and Nam Ou rivers in Laos, and the Puyuan River in Sipsong Panna, southern China. Specific locations include Ban Pak Ing, Chiang Khong and Ban Jam Pong, Wiang Kaen in Thailand; Ban Pak Soeng and Ban Hat Kho in Luang Prabang Province, Laos; and Manbian, Muang Lun, Chiang Rung in Yunnan.

Inland wetland communities where the riparian environment has undergone rapid change include the Lao community of Ban Thung Ang and the Thai community of San Sai Ngam, Chiang Rai Province. In these communities, reservoirs have been reclaimed and riverine forest destroyed for agricultural purposes. These changes not only deprive migrating fish of spawning sites, but also bring about the degradation of local cultures and livelihoods. Indigenous knowledge and practices retained by riverine people are vulnerable to external socioeconomic impacts. How local inhabitants perceive of and utilize their natural resources for sustainable livelihoods is an urgent topic for investigation. Research sites include Ban San Xai Mun, Thoeng District and Ban Ta Luang, Phya Mengrai in Thailand.

Upland ethnic communities where upland fish resources are a significant part of local diets and protein inputs include the Mien and Hmong communities in Thoeng District, Chiang Rai. Highlanders in the mountains of the Ing River watershed have depended not only upon hill farms and forest environments for their livelihoods, but their health and diet also depends upon upstream fish resources. With the introduction of cash crops and market economy, the lives of these highlanders are undergoing rapid change. Shifting cultivation is no longer practicable, and indigenous knowledge and practices used in agriculture, hunting, and gathering are fast disappearing. To what extent these external influences affect local cultures and societies are crucial factors in evaluating prospects for a sustainable future. Inquiries into interactions between riparian and mountain peoples in terms of subsistence practices and local dietary systems is also crucial for our understanding of marginal highlanders' adaptive responses to change. Research sites in this category include Ban Khun Huai Khrai, Thoeng District in Thailand, and Ban Suan Luang, Luang Prabang Province in Laos.

What are the impacts of transnational infrastructure development, especially the construction of hydroelectric dams in China and the blasting of shoals and reefs for commercial navigation, on local ecosystems and fish stocks, household and village economies, health and dietary systems, and rules and ritual practices governing natural resource management in these four types of ecosystems? What are the adaptive responses of marginal groups in the Mekong Basin to increasing transnationalization and environmental degradation? For instance, is the decline in riparian resources leading to increasing forest destruction? How is environmental change related to increasing migration, forest destruction, and the maintenance of community-based resource management practices?

This book seeks to understand the impact of subregional growth and development on resource use, class differentiation, lifestyles, and cultures, and to identify serious health, economic, and environmental threats caused by unbalanced development within and across countries. It seeks to enhance public understanding and awareness of the trans-boundary impacts of subregional development on the lives of the greater Mekong peoples and their environments. It seeks to identify indigenous knowledge and practices regarding the use of aquatic and agro-forestry resources, as a step towards finding alternative and more sustainable development paths.

To achieve these objectives, this book adheres to three guiding concepts. *Transnational enclosure* guides us in an attempt to look at globalization as an uneven economic process which creates a fragmented and uneven distribution of resources between various groups and sectors in developing countries. *Ethnoecology* frames the importance of local knowledge in sustainable development. A focus on *civil society* or "globalization from below"—mobilizing highly specific local, national, and regional groups on matters of equity, access, justice, and redistribution—implies a need to design and support cross-scale institutional linkages in the Mekong Basin. The meanings and usages of these guiding concepts are further explained below.

Transnational Enclosure

Globalization is becoming a major source of anxiety within the public spheres of many societies in the developing world. What does globalization mean for labor markets and agricultural production? How will globalization affect the ability of nations to determine the economic futures of their populations? Which parts of the nation-state are protectors of stakeholder communities and which parts are direct affiliates of global capital? How will globalization affect the ability of local communities to sustainably manage their natural resources in an increasingly deterritorialized world? Anthropologist Arjun Appadurai (2001, 2) suggests that underlying these important questions is the sense that social exclusion is closely linked to theories of knowledge that exclude, and a concern that the discourses of expertise that are setting the rules for global transactions and development have left ordinary people outside and behind. The Mekong Basin is a fine case in point.

Despite a longstanding interest in the Mekong Basin's resources and the rapid pace of economic development in the region, the basin is still often seen by various governments as underdeveloped in terms of its potential. Over the past decades, constraints on resource development have included Cold War confrontations and limited access to investment capital needed for large-scale development projects. These constraints are now disappearing. Recent political rapprochement, coupled with rapid economic growth within the region, has created increasing pressure for rapid exploitation of the Mekong Basin resource base, culminating in a series of dams, highways, and waterways for commercial navigation currently under planning and construction.

In theory, according to the Asian Development Bank (ADB 2000) transition toward more market-oriented regimes is an important factor contributing to the viability of economic cooperation in the Mekong Basin. Regional economic reforms that began in the 1990s have created an environment conducive to increased trade and investment and other forms of economic cooperation. Economies of scale and specialization resulting from subregional cooperation facilitate investment in Mekong Basin countries as a whole, exceeding individual countries' abilities to attract investors. By generating economic synergy and dynamism, subregional cooperation contributes to the goal of sustained economic growth in individual countries, and helps improve living conditions of the poor and improve people's overall quality of life.

In reality, however, the implications of large-scale development in the Mekong Basin are diverse and complex. While potential economic returns from increased exploitation of natural resources are great, the socioeconomic and environmental risks are also very high. The ecological and social consequences of development projects such as the construction of a series of dams on the Mekong, are scarcely considered in the discourse of state and interstate fora. More importantly, the benefits of development are not shared evenly among all social groups and stakeholders, creating a fragmented and uneven distribution of resources in Mekong Basin countries. The factors behind this uneven development include unequal levels of development within and between countries, social hierarchies leading to skewed access to resources, and the current thrust of globalization which tends to place economic growth before equity and sustainability in most countries' development agendas.

To some extent, the Mekong is an open-pool resource to which a large number of actors have access. Overuse of this resource, particularly through the development of a series of hydroelectric dams and commercial navigation, creates problems which threaten to destroy the system's overall sustainability. The fish population may collapse, the flow of water may decline, and the fertility of seasonally flooded lands may be reduced. Each country in the Mekong Basin faces a decision about how much of the basin's resources to use: how much water to be dammed, how many acres of forest land to be cut. If all countries practice restraint, the basin's resources can be sustained. But this is a development dilemma. If a country limits its use of natural resources and its neighbors do not, then the resource base will still collapse and the country that practices restraint loses the short-term benefits of taking its share.

Consequently, most countries in the Mekong Basin put economic growth and resource exploitation before equity and sustainability on their development agendas. They also see clearly that the market is the best mechanism for facilitating development in a globalized world. The market economy requires the state to adopt private property systems and institutions, so that resources such as water, land, and forest are transferable, inheritable, and have enforceable regulations. Secure property systems lead to increased productivity and more efficient use and management of resources, which translates into economic growth and development. Even a former Communist country like China has transformed its development agenda to a market-based economy. With financial support from international development banks and institutions, various governments in the Mekong Basin have embarked upon a process of privatization, decentralization, and clarification of property regimes in order to facilitate market-based development. In the Mekong Basin, the expansion of market economies has led to the transnational enclosure of the Mekong Basin's resources.

The term "enclosure" (*The Ecologist* 1992, 132) was first used to describe a historical process which took place in England between the fifteenth and nineteenth centuries when feudal lords gradually claimed ownership over communal land formerly used by serfs. Enclosure played a supporting role in the transition from feudal to capitalist modes of production, producing a vast number of landless peasants who were forced to migrate into cities and work as low-wage laborers. Enclosure in England did not merely involve a transfer of power from the commons to the expropriating elite, but signaled a more profound change in the social order in two related respects. By redefining natural resources as "property," enclosure gave it the status of a commodity, tradable in a rapidly expanding market system. Secondly, enclosure was justified by its perpetrators and apologists as "improvement," which was seen as linked with profit in the same way that the later term "development" has come to be associated with "progress" and "economic growth."

In the contemporary world, enclosure is closely related to government development and territorialization policies. In Thailand, for instance, the government centralizes its development efforts and imposes development plans that enable the industrial sector to benefit from cheap resources and labor from the agricultural sector in flagging rural areas. One clear case was promotion of eucalyptus plantations in the 1990s (Yos 1996). The Thai government targeted large areas, formerly used for farming by many peasant households, for eucalyptus plantations, and gave concessions to private firms resulting in the creation of a massive number of dispossessed peasants.

The concept of transnational enclosure is employed here to refer to an increasingly centralized decision-making process which enables the state and commercial interests to gain control of territories that have traditionally been used and cherished by local peoples in the Mekong Basin, transforming these areas into expendable resources for exploitation. Enclosure tears people from their rivers, lands, and forests; removes these natural resources along with accompanying knowledge and cosmologies from the cultural framework in which they have been embedded; and forces them into a new framework which reinforces the values and interests of the state and dominant groups. In this sense, the Mekong and its tributaries are dis-embedded from local fabrics of self-reliance, redefined as "state property," transformed into exploitable economic resources, and turned into a series of dams and waterways for commercial navigation and trade.

Having transformed the Mekong into a "resource" for national and transnational production and development, enclosure assigns control over this resource to actors outside local communities. Enclosure reorganizes societies to meet the overriding demands of the market and ushers in a new political order. When the environment is turned over to new uses, a new set of rules and new forms of organization are required. Enclosure redefines how the environment is managed, by whom and for whose benefit. By enclosing the Mekong, states tear it from the fabric of local control, the breakdown of which sets the course for the degradation of natural resources.

Local control is essential for sustainable resource management and preservation for at least three reasons. The first is that the environment itself is local. Nature diversifies itself into separate niches, intertwining local environment in its own intricate web of interdependence relations. Given this fact, the environment is best managed by local communities that nourish local differences. The second reason is that where people rely directly on their natural environment for their livelihoods, they develop an intimate local knowledge of the environment which informs their consciousness and actions.

Local knowledge is, by nature, confined to a specific locality or set of ecosystems; highly localized and situated. Its focus is the complex web of relationships between humans, animals, fish, plants, insects, natural forces, spirits, and landscapes within a particular locality or ecosystem. Local knowledge develops in the context of this interaction and inter-dependence between complex webs of relationships. For this reason, it is based on a profound understanding of human-environmental rela-tionships. Profound understanding leads to the ability to administer, modify, utilize, and develop resources in a sustainable manner. Many fishing communities in the Mekong Basin have developed elaborate management practices which reflect a thorough understanding of the interactions between fish ecology and the seasonal fluctuation of water and food supplies. Conscious management and ritual practices dictate periods of abstention from fishing so that adequate migration of fish to their spawning grounds is ensured. In this sense, local control—based on the local knowledge of various communities in the Mekong basin— over small niches within the Mekong is extremely important for sustainable management of the river as a whole.

The third reason why local control is essential has to do with checks and balances. The remarkable success of local communities in safeguarding their environments is well documented. In northern Thailand (Yos 2003a), the management of community forests by various ethnic groups based on their cultural practices has proven much more effective than management of forests by the state. This success depends not only on local knowledge and ritual practices, but also on cultural checks and balances that impose moral responsibility, thereby limiting potential abuses of the environment. In this sense, the expansion of centralized control by the state entails a shrinking space for community-based resource management and eventually leads to a complete denial of local rights.

Adopting transnational enclosure as a guiding concept helps us to understand a major development dilemma in the Mekong Basin: how to keep a sense of balance between economic growth and environmental crisis, between the global market and local needs, and between centralization and local control over resource management. Recognition of the importance of local control leads us to the vital necessity of maintaining local knowledge. This can only be achieved when local peoples are no longer forced to abandon their customary management practices because of dispossession, intrusion by external forces, or degradation of the ecosystems upon which they ultimately depend. The maintenance of local knowledge therefore requires respect for the rights of local people to use and manage their own resources.

Situated Knowledge

In a seminal paper published in 1961, Harold Conklin (1961) introduced "the ethnoecological approach" that was to dismantle the dominant view of shifting cultivation as a primitive and destructive agricultural system. Over the years, ethnoecology has represented a serious attempt to understand the logic, complexity, and sophistication of the local knowledge of various peoples throughout the world.

From an ethnoecological perspective, local knowledge is a repertoire of situated experience developed in particular physical and cultural contexts, from intimate interactions between humans and the environment. It is culturally embedded in its local context, and grounded in particular physical territories. Local knowledge should not, however, be represented as being in opposition to modern knowledge by employing a range of binary concepts: local versus scientific knowledge, traditional versus modern knowledge, and folk versus universal knowledge. Rather, the focus on local knowledge represents a shift away from preoccupation with centralized, technically-oriented solutions to development problems that have failed to improve the prospects of most of the world's peasants and small farmers. As political scientist Arun Agrawal (1995) more recently notes, by highlighting the possible contribution to be made by knowledge in the hands of the marginalized poor, the local knowledge concept focuses both attention and resources on those who most need them.

Over the past two decades, popular trends in studies of local knowledge (Merchant 1992, Hoffman 1997, Nygren 1999, Yos 2003a) have included advocating the role of local knowledge in addressing the global environmental crisis, and seeing human activities as heading for a collision with nature. Many scholars maintain the superiority of local knowledge systems because they represent a close affinity with nature, while others like Agrawal have argued for dismantling the divide between local and scientific knowledge.

In this book, local knowledge is defined as the knowledge used by local people to make a living in a changing environment. Knowledge production is seen as a process of social negotiation involving multiple actors and complex power relations. Local knowledge involves change, adaptation, and dynamism, with diverse social actors engaged in a process of contesting and reinterpreting. Local knowledge should therefore be viewed as a continuous process (Yos 2003a, 43), where traditional and modern, situational and hybrid, local and global coexist and are mingled together to create a complicated ethnoecological reality.

The ethnoecological approach, with its emphasis on local knowledge, is employed here as a conceptual tool to understand how local communities in the Mekong Basin have learned to live with their diverse ecosystems; how they have developed sophisticated knowledge about resource management, how local knowledge is reordered, rearranged, and repositioned to meet the changing needs of modern times.

Over the past decade, increasing transnational cooperation in infrastructure development and freer cross-border flows of people and commerce has posed serious challenges to local community livelihoods and environments. Forest and aquatic resources are two of the most important sources of nutrition and income for over 55 million people living within the six riparian countries of the Mekong Basin, providing the bulk of this population's protein requirements. Forest and aquatic resources thus stand out as a central issue to livelihood development and a major area of risk should the Mekong Basin's delicate ecosystems be disturbed. Different sectoral interests pose key resource management challenges for both the Mekong Basin as a whole, and for individual countries. The need for energy and foreign exchange generated by hydroelectric dams sits uneasily with biodiversity conservation and the maintenance of aquatic resources. Forestry and local agricultural livelihoods come into conflict in many parts of the Mekong Basin, and deforestation is another key threat to environmental integrity. There are also incompatibilities between vegetation clearance in upper watersheds, whether from forestry, the spread of rubber plantations, or shifting cultivation; and questions about the sustainability of hydroelectric investments due to erosion and siltation. Impacts of current patterns of resource use and development vary from group to group, giving rise to resource competition and conflict between different socio-political actors.

By investigating the rapid socioeconomic changes that many marginal groups in the Mekong Basin are currently facing, this book aims to explore the dynamism of local ecological knowledge and its potential to modify, shift, transform, and reshape new systems of meaning as adaptive responses of these marginal communities to change. The dynamism of local knowledge takes place within the development context as a means of adaptation to socioeconomic and environmental change. It signifies a continuous process of transformation, involving breaks, ruptures, interruptions, and reorganization, during which local knowledge is reordered, rearranged, and repositioned to provide new forms of knowledge in order to articulate new historical realities. In this light, the book argues for a need to incorporate a new bottom-up planning process in the development of the Mekong Basin which must be adopted in future approaches to regional resource management. Stakeholder approaches to development, based on recognition of the value of local knowledge, provide an underlying framework for inclusiveness and participation, taking into consideration the unequal political, social, and economic power structures in and between countries involved. The issue of unequal power relations in and between countries in the Mekong Basin brings us to the concept of civil society, with a particular focus on local empowerment, and interactions across scale from the local level upwards.

Global Civil Society and Cross-Scale Institutional Linkages

While global capital and the system of nation-states negotiate the terms of the emergent world order, an international order of institutions has emerged that bears witness to what Arjun Appadurai (2001) calls "grassroots globalization" or "globalization from below." It is conceived of as a conglomeration of non-state, non-economic global practices and institutions that provides a counterbalance to the increasingly integrated power of a world system ruled by nation-states and transnational capital (Barnet and Cavanagh 1994, 429–430).

The worldwide bourgeoning of non-governmental organizations (NGOs) mobilized around specific local, national, and regional groups on matters of equity, access, justice, social needs, and values appears to be a natural institutional embodiment of the liberal conception of the term. NGOs have complex relations with the state, the public, and local communities. They are at times complicit with state policies and at other times violently opposed to these policies. In many countries of the Mekong Basin, especially Thailand, NGOs have their roots in the student and popular democracy and civil rights movements over the last three decades. NGOs provide a legitimate arena for social transformation and resistance motivated by political concern for people who are relatively disadvantaged within the world system. Some NGOs are part of transnational advocacy networks, their practices and strategies global. Hence, they are one of the most important institutional instruments in the effort to globalize from below (Appadurai 2001, 17–18).

In many developing countries, globalization is creating increasing inequality both within and across countries, as well as furthering the rapid exploitation of natural resources and ecological degradation. Global capital in its current form is characterized by strategies of predatory mobility that have immensely compromised the capacities of people in a single location to even recognize, much less understand or resist these strategies. NGOs, too, often lack the vision, planning, and brute energy of capital to globalize through the capture of markets and the control of media. Those critical voices which represent the marginalized, poor, and dispossessed in international arenas in which global policies are made, often lack the means to articulate a systematic grasp of the complexities of globalization. A major challenge to the social sciences is to seriously commit to the study of globalization from below. An effort to compare and describe the complex set of relationships between globalization from above and globalization from below could contribute to new forms of pedagogy that could level the theoretical playing field for grassroots activists in international arenas.

Over the past decade, the development and management of the Mekong has been characterized by centralized, top-down planning and action by states, without public consultation or participation. The process has failed to integrate the multiple values and objectives held by the various stakeholders involved in river basin management. For civil society or grassroots globalization, community management and control based on locally situated knowledge is the key solution to better governance (Miller and Hirsch 2003, 8). In practice, however, neither purely local level management nor purely higher level management works well by itself. Rather, there is a need to design and support cross-scale management, linking institutions both horizontally—particularly at the local level—and vertically, that is both nationally and internationally). Still, cross-scale institutional linkage (Berkes 2002) means something more than management at several scales, isolated from one another. It requires processes of negotiation at multiple levels: negotiation over water itself, negotiation over water rights, and negotiation over the most appropriate model of river basin development. It also requires an increased role for grassroots globalization in actions and decisions around river basin development. The scope of such cross-scale institutional linkages is local to international, focusing on links between local institutions and higher level government entities.

The concept of grassroots globalization allows us to explore the increasing role of local and international NGOs in negotiation, conflict resolution, and action on issues of the most appropriate model of Mekong Basin development; to compare and describe a complex picture of the relationship between globalization from above and below in the Mekong Basin; to discuss the possibility of establishing cross-scale institutional linkages, including co-management arrangements; and to identify promising institutional forms for cross-level institutional linkages.

This book is divided into seven chapters. The first chapter describes the Mekong Basin, its bio-geographical zones, and recent conflicting claims over its rich natural resources. Chapter two elaborates on the transnational enclosure of the Mekong by various states, especially China and Thailand. Chapters three to five provide brief ethnographic accounts of riparian communities in Chiang Rung, Luang Prabang, and northern Thailand, respectively. Through investigating the rapid ecological and socioeconomic change that many riparian communities in Yunnan, Laos, and Thailand are currently facing, this book contends that the potential for environmental damage in the Mekong Basin has dramatically increased over the past decade.

Chapter six describes how large-scale development projects also have adverse effects on local cultures, lifestyles and subsistence practices.

Consequently, local riparian communities must find new ways and means to adapt their knowledge and cultural practices to cope with changing environmental and socioeconomic contexts. This chapter also examines the flexible adaptability of local knowledge and its potential to modify and reshape new systems of meaning as local responses of these marginal communities to change. Finally, chapter seven explores the relationship between transboundary environmental problems and the rise of transnational civil society in the Mekong Basin. The book contends that an emerging transnational civil society could serve as a forum in which the voices of all stakeholders are heard and a negotiated space of good governance and participation in the true sense of comanagement of natural resources between local, national, and international agencies is realized.

ONE

The Mekong Basin

The Mekong River and its many tributaries are the essence of the natural wealth of the region's communities. These tributaries and their associated ecosystems form the foundation of local livelihood security and economies in various parts of Yunnan, Laos, Burma, Thailand, Cambodia, and Vietnam. The importance of the Mekong River, its tributaries, and wetlands, is embedded in the local knowledge and belief systems, rituals, music, and art of its indigenous peoples. In recent years, however, the Mekong has increasingly been disembedded from local fabrics of self-reliance, and transformed into an exploitable economic resource for national and transnational production and development.

The top-down management of the Mekong Basin takes place within two conflicting sets of boundaries. The first set is political boundaries resulting from the division of the region into geobody political entities such as countries and provinces. The second set is biophysical boundaries or different sets of ecosystems. This conflict bears both on socioeconomic data which is collected and analyzed by artificial politico-administrative units rather than by natural entities, and on natural resource management, which is similarly constrained by political boundaries that divide watersheds and biophysical zones (Hirsch and Choeng 1966).

Historically, the six countries of the Mekong Basin have been entangled in ideological tension and conflicts. During the Cold War years, the river was an axis of division rather than unity. The subsidence of Cold War tensions in the region in the 1990s brought significant changes. Recent events have seen a stronger Chinese presence, convergence of development orientation among the riparian countries, and increasing pressures for Mekong resource development.

With a length of about 4,200 kilometers, the Mekong River is one the longest rivers in Southeast Asia. The river's watershed is composed of an upper and a lower basin. This division is topographical, but since the early 1950s, it has also been influenced by geopolitical factors that have played an influential role in the Mekong Basin. Beginning in 1957, Laos, Thailand, Cambodia, and Vietnam sought to establish and maintain a Mekong resource regime through the device of the Mekong Committee. From that time on, the institutional basis for natural resource management at the basin level, and subsequent investigations of possibilities for coordinating development in the areas of hydro-electricity, irrigation, flood control, drainage, navigation, watershed management, and water supply, were all maintained and modified through this regime. In all these areas, the Mekong Committee served as an avenue through which financial and technical assistance for development could be delivered.

Built upon a form of interdependence, the regime encouraged limited cooperation in order to support lasting cooperation. Such assurance of longevity was deemed essential if international financing was to be secured for member countries. Given increasing conflicts in the region in the 1960s resulting from the Vietnam War and related ideological confrontations, the regime was also underwritten by strong political objectives, securing mutual respect for mutual restraint. This was embedded in a veto rule which required that all activities in the entire river basin be approved by all riparian states.

The Mekong Committee's regime was nevertheless marked by the turbulent political context of its day. Military conflict and social upheavals limited the extent to which resources were developed within this framework. Cambodia's withdrawal in 1975 and the establishment of an Interim Mekong Committee further slowed the pace of joint development. But the flagging vision for Mekong subregionalism and its many possibilities was dramatically revived with the establishment of the Mekong River Commission (MRC) in April of 1995, following the signing of an Agreement of Cooperation for the Sustainable Development of the Mekong River Basin by Laos, Thailand, Cambodia, and Vietnam.

The MRC consists of a Council, a Joint Committee, and a Secretariat. The latter, in particular, is quite similar in structure to that existing under the Mekong Committee. A significant change from the 1957 Committee rules is that downstream countries no longer have an effective veto on upstream developments. Rules are structured around notification and consultation projects that affect dry and wet season water flows. In the case of tributaries, prior consultation and maintenance of the natural minimum water flow is required during the dry season. During the wet season, projects concerning tributaries require "notification" only.

As one commentator on post-Cold War Mekong resource politics rightly observes (Makim 2002), the new Mekong regime strongly reflects Thai preferences for the structure of political action in the Mekong subregion. This is broadly evidenced by the general requirements of the new Article 5 ("Reasonable and Equitable Utilisation") of the 1995 general arrangements for water sharing in the Mekong. Whereas the original arrangements required prior notification for all projects throughout the entire river basin without seasonal variation, and contained a related comprehensive veto mechanism, the new and much weaker arrangements require prior notification and unanimity only for projects affecting the mainstream Mekong, and are also subject to seasonal variation.

This change is particularly disadvantageous to the downstream states of Laos, Cambodia, and Vietnam. Not only does it limit obligations among the co-riparian states, it also circumscribes power within the regime, returning it instead to individual sovereign states. While resource development in upstream Thailand might have transboundary impacts, downstream states have a reduced capacity to know of or influence these activities through the auspices of the MRC regime.

The question of transboundary impacts reminds us of the issue of membership for the Upper Mekong Basin riparian states, especially

China. Upstream China is now a major player in the region. China holds extensive plans for the Upper Mekong's development and has already built two dams across the mainstream, with two more under construction and four more being projected. China tends toward unilateralism and has undertaken only cautious and very limited involvement with the MRC. The issue of membership for China, along with Burma, thus raises serious possibilities for the reemergence of contention among co-riparian states in the Mekong region.

The Basin's Bio-Geographical Zones

The primary biophysical boundary division within the Mekong watershed is that of upper and lower basin. The Upper Mekong Basin, which falls within the territory of China, spans a wide range of altitudes, latitudes, climates, and vegetation zones. The Lower Mekong Basin covers a somewhat narrower range of biogeographical zones. The five lower riparian countries—Burma, Laos, Thailand, Cambodia, and Vietnam—contain almost 80 percent of the entire basin area and account for more than four-fifths of the water that passes through the basin each year. The Lower Basin is monsoonal and marked by great seasonal variation in rainfall. High season flows are typically fifteen times that of low season flows, and this fluctuation is a defining characteristic of the basin's physical conditions. According to Hirsch and Cheong (1996), the Mekong Basin can be distinguished into a total of seven bio-geographical zones.

1. UPPER MEKONG. The section of the Mekong (Lancang) Basin in China is characterized by steep, narrow gorges. The elongated shape of the Upper Mekong catchments means that tributaries are short and tend to flow directly into the river. Rainfall is significantly lower than in other parts of the basin and is less marked by seasonal variation. Tributary watersheds include high mountainous terrain leading down from the Tibetan plateau, to steep topography in Yunnan Province. Agricultural practices in lower Yunnan, especially in Xishuangbanna, are based on both terraced wet rice farming and shifting cultivation on hillsides. Due to the incised nature of the topography, little large scale irrigation

development is envisaged. From 1986 onwards, China began a project to build eight hydroelectric dams and two reservoirs on the Lancang in Yunnan. Most hydroelectric development on the Lancang is likely to be on the main stream.

2. NORTHERN HIGHLANDS. This section of the Mekong Basin covers the highlands of Burma, northern Thailand, and northern Laos. The northern highlands are marked by several large tributaries, including the Nam Khan, Nam Ou, Nam Sueng, and Nam Ngum in Laos, the Mae Kok in Burma and Thailand, and the Nam Ing in Thailand. Forest cover has been reduced considerably in this zone. Steep slopes combined with forest clearance lead to high rates of soil erosion. Agriculture is based on shifting cultivation, interspersed with small pockets of wet rice cultivation. Opium production is an important source of cash income for various ethnic communities. The Northern Highlands has been earmarked for a number of hydroelectric dams in Burma, Thailand, and Laos. There is also a planned inter-basin diversion scheme from the Kok and Ing tributaries to the Chao Phraya Basin in central Thailand.

3. EASTERN HIGHLANDS. The Mekong's Eastern Highlands form the eastern part of central and southern Laos, the western part of Vietnam's Central Highlands, and a small part of eastern Cambodia. Rainfall is highest in this part of the basin, and tributaries originating in this section contribute about two-fifths of the entire basin's water. The eastern highlands are also marked by heavily forested areas, extremely rich in biological diversity. Agriculture is based on rotational swidden farming practiced by various ethnic groups. Large areas in Vietnam have also been cleared and settled by Kinh lowlanders planting upland cash crops. Several large hydroelectric dams are projected in Laos and Vietnam.

4. THE KORAT PLATEAU. This section of the Mekong Basin covers northeastern Thailand and the left bank of the Mekong plains in Laos. The Korat Plateau is drained by the Mun and Chi rivers and other smaller tributaries flowing directly into the Mekong. This part of the Mekong is the driest area of the basin, with low rainfall and poor soil fertility. Nevertheless, the gentle topography has contributed to a

relatively high population density compared with the highlands. Agriculture is thus extensive and forest cover has been cleared for wet rice cultivation and cash crop production, especially cassava, corn, and other dry-land cultivars. The Korat Plateau is facing major water and land resource problems due to saline intrusion. A number of large-scale projects have been proposed for the area, notably the Kong-Chi-Mun intra-basin diversion project, which could have a direct impact on water flows in downstream countries.

5. SOUTHERN UPLANDS. The uplands of southern Cambodia form the southwestern rim of the Mekong Basin. This area is drained by rivers flowing northward into the Great Lake (Tonle Sap) and by the Prek Thnot River flowing north directly into the Bassac, one of the Mekong's two main distributaries in Cambodia. Rainfall is above average on the southern side of these uplands. A hydroelectric dam is projected for the Prek Thnot River.

6. LOWLANDS. The Mekong lowlands form a large portion of the northern half of Cambodia and extend into southern Laos and eastern Thailand. The river itself is broken into highlands and lowlands at the Khone Falls, a substantial navigational obstacle but a site of great significance in terms of aquatic biodiversity. Another feature of immense importance in terms of ecology and natural resources is the Tonle Sap. During the peak monsoon period of each year, the Tonle Sap River draining the lake reverses its flow, giving the water body a key role in regulating water flows. The Tonle Sap region also forms the agricultural heartland of Cambodia and produces a large portion of the country's food protein through its abundance of fisheries. The major agricultural practice is wet rice farming.

7. DELTA. The Mekong Delta, a triangular area of southeastern Cambodia and southern Vietnam, is by far the most densely populated part of the basin, with a population of some 15 million people on about 50,000 square kilometers of fertile soil. Natural levees separate the river from depressions that are subject to flooding during the wet season. Agriculture in the delta is dominated by wet rice farming, which has been adapted to deep water and saline conditions. The Mekong Delta is

Vietnam's rice bowl, providing food security for the whole country and contributing to Vietnam's status as the world's leading exporter of rice. However, the delta is facing serious water and land resource problems, including acute flooding, acid sulphate solids, saline intrusion, and water contamination due to prawn farming in mangrove forests.

Natural Resources in the Mekong Basin

For centuries, the majority of resource users and managers in the Mekong Basin have been farmers and fisherfolk whose livelihoods depended directly on the diverse and abundant food supply they extracted from the local environment. The basin supports a wide range of farming systems, many of which are still primarily subsistence oriented, and only weakly linked to the market economy. These areas include the more remote parts of northern Laos, Cambodia, Yunnan, the Vietnamese highlands, and even parts of northeastern Thailand and the Delta. Penetration of the cash economy and market-oriented production, especially in terms of monocultural production of cash crops and various forms of contract farming, has recently led to rapid commodification of the basin's resource base. The trend toward more market-oriented production has serious implications for natural resource management as forests, land, and water become valued commodities, placing added pressure on them and accentuating the impacts of poorly defined property regimes and tenurial arrangements. As a result, many subsistence farmers find themselves under increasing pressure from commercial production.

In addition to a growing trend toward market-oriented agriculture culminating in increasing tension between subsistence and commercial production, there is also an inherent conflict between upland and lowland production systems throughout the Mekong Basin. Ethnic groups who have practised shifting cultivation for centuries are now faced with a rapidly changing environment in which to carry out their livelihoods. As powerful demands for resources, land, and military control have guided state expansion into the most remote corners of the region, the autonomy and mobility of marginal cultural groups in once inaccessible places—tropical forests and rugged mountains—are increasingly threatened. In fact, over the past decade, many ethnic minority groups in the subregion have been victimized by a militant conservation policy to protect watershed areas. Various Mekong Basin states have strengthened their forest conservation policies by establishing national parks, forest reserves, and reforestation areas, and by stepping up relocation schemes. The rapid expansion of conservation forests through the establishment of national parks and reforestation programs has threatened the security of tenure of shifting cultivators who typically have only customary access to forestland, in many cases leading to declining fallow periods and increased soil erosion. Lowland farmers have moreover come into serious conflict with highland shifting cultivators in many parts of the region as pressure has mounted on upper watersheds, and resource competition, especially for water, has become more intense.

In recent years, shifting cultivators in the Mekong Basin have been blamed for the destruction of forests and the degradation of highland areas. Despite the fact that several recent studies (Grandstaff 1980, Warner 1991, Walker 1992, Woranoot 1998) on ethnic groups who practice shifting cultivation argue that shifting cultivation results from selection and adjustment processes appropriate to ecosystems in upper altitudes of the tropical zone, and rests on a basis of profound ecological knowledge and sustainable management, shifting cultivators and "slash and burn" practices have invariably been the focus of many government "stabilization" programs seeking alternative upland development. But the rapid expansion of centralized control over natural resource management in the Mekong Basin is not only limited to upland development. On the contrary, the effective development and management of the basin is viewed more as a matter of sustaining economic growth. Technical and engineering works, action plans and policy agendas, are all largely developed in the absence of public consultation and participation.

The population of the Mekong Basin is mainly agrarian-based with rice the major crop. The wide range of agricultural practices employed throughout the subregion reflects differences in ecosystems, ethnicity, soil conditions, climate, and levels of mechanization. While there is much hyperbole about growth and industrial development in various Mekong Basin countries, economies are still largely resource-based, and agriculture continues to be the prime economic activity in the basin for the foreseeable future. While many agricultural intensification programs include aspects of poverty eradication, fairer land distribution, and extension services, impacts in terms of social justice are often mixed. In fact, agricultural intensification programs in both upland and lowland areas (see Phrek 1993, Naiyana 2001, Dien 2002, and Samata 2003) often lead to increasing internal differentiation, monocultural production, soil erosion, excessive agrochemical use, and gender inequality. Development of the agricultural economy of the basin also depends to a large extent on the construction of irrigation projects by highly centralized state agencies.

Over the past decade, high rates of economic growth in Mekong Basin countries have coincided with a high rate of forest destruction and environmental degradation. The amount of forest cover in the Lower Mekong Basin varies widely. Laos and Cambodia retain the largest proportion of forest cover, while Thailand and Vietnam retain the smallest. The Central Highlands of Vietnam is the most heavily forested area, with forests covering 60 percent, representing almost half of Vietnam's timber reserves. Vietnam on the whole retains only 20 percent of its forests compared to 43 percent for Thailand, 55 percent for Laos, and 71 percent for Cambodia (Hirsch and Choeng 1996). Figures show that large portions of forests have been destroyed in the Lower Basin countries, and that current rates of forest destruction are not sustainable. Although logging bans have been imposed in most of these countries in recognition of the destructive impacts of a largely uncontrolled timber industry, these bans have been invariably ineffectual, and illegal logging still occurs in many areas, with little effort put into reforestation. Placing the blame on shifting cultivators often does not lead to a real understanding of the many forces stimulating forest destruction: population pressure, agricultural expansion, corruption, government economic planning and construction of megaprojects, and, especially in Burma, the exigencies of war and ethnic conflict.

Perhaps one of the most important resources in the Mekong Basin is the rich river fauna. Many of the fish found in the Mekong are migratory and travel far upstream or downstream in search of food and spawning grounds (Poulsen and Sinthavong 2003). *Pla beuk*, the Mekong giant catfish, for instance, is said to migrate from Cambodia to Lake Urhai in Dali, Yunnan, to spawn. More than 90 percent of fish production in the Lower Mekong Basin is from capture fisheries in the Mekong and its tributaries. The total production is unknown but estimated to be from 1.0 to 3.1 million tons (Jensen 1996, Bush 2003). In using production figures, it is important to note that subsistence and small-scale fisheries are underrepresented in many countries and this unaccounted for production is vital to the livelihood of large rural populations in the basin. Fish is the primary source of animal protein and comprises more than half the total animal protein intake in the region. As such, any disruption to production would have significant nutritional consequences, particularly for the basin's poorer inhabitants.

While migratory fish are important in the Mekong River, A study by Hill and Hill (Mekong Secretariat 1994), notes that impacts of hydropower schemes are difficult to ascertain due to limited information on fish biology and ecology. The most serious impact of hydropower development is the blockage of fish migration—proposed fish ladders notwithstanding—which could cause a wholesale decline in fisheries throughout the Lower Mekong Basin. Fisheries are one of the most important livelihood activities for people in the Mekong Basin (See Poulsen and Sinthavong 2003, Visser and Poulsen 2003, Bush 2003). Fishing in the Mekong River and its tributaries is most prevalent in the dry season, while in the rainy season people generally fish in wetlands, streams, ponds, and inundated rice fields. The best fishing areas in the Mekong and its tributaries are rapids, where the river's flow over a stratum of rock is relatively fast and shallow, and connects deep water pools and stretches of seasonally inundated forest.

The major fish migration of each year commences at the beginning of the rainy season. When the rains begin in May, streams begin to flow and the water level and volume of many tributaries begins to rise. At that time, a large number of fish species begin migrating from the Mekong to large and small tributaries, and local villagers in riparian communities are able to catch large amounts of fish that provide a sizable income. After the fish migrations at the beginning of the monsoon season have taken place, there is considerable fishing activity in the wetlands for the duration of the rainy season, but no important fisheries in the Mekong or large tributaries during this time of the year. In October, as the rainy season ends, an important fishery based on migrating fishes of the small species of *cyprinids* identified collectively by local fishers as *pla soi* are caught in various parts of Laos and Thailand. At this time, fish also move out of rice fields, streams, lakes and inundated depressions to return to the main tributaries. This is the time when villagers make barrier traps at the edges of rice fields and in streams to catch fish. In many cases, large quantities of fish are caught. Fishing in natural inland depressions is extremely important for people living in those communities situated away from the Mekong and its larger tributaries as it is only during this period that many of these fish can be caught in locations away from the rivers. Ethnic Lao and Lue villagers employ a number of traditional practices to catch fish, including trapping wild fish in ponds when flood waters recede and communal fishing in wetland areas. These systems are dependent upon the seasonal flood cycle of the Mekong River system.

The relative importance of fisheries to local communities may be increasing, especially in areas where rice production does not provide families with a sufficient supply of food for the entire year. In these cases, wild capture fisheries in the Mekong and its tributaries are the main means of livelihood and fisheries are becoming a significant component of local economies. Fish traders from Luang Prabang in Laos and Chiang Khong in Thailand travel to riverside villages to buy fish on a regular basis. Some riverside villages sell hundreds of kilograms or more per day. In various areas, villagers sell their own fish directly at market centers, with marketing patterns varying from place to place.

In addition to fish, many other aquatic resources are gathered from rivers and wetlands by villagers, although the amounts and types of resources harvested differ from village to village. These aquatic resources include shrimp, snails, weeds, frogs, crabs, and edible insects. While these aquatic resources are mainly collected for daily consumption by local villagers, a great deal of income can be realized from their sale.

The cultivation of riverbank vegetable crops (Blake 2003) along the Mekong and many of its tributaries is also a very important livelihood activity for villagers in Yunnan, Laos, and Thailand. Produce from riverbank gardens contributes to family food supplies while the surplus is sold at local markets. In various parts of Laos and Thailand, there are two overlapping seasons for riverbank cropping, the first from August to December, and the second starting in December with crops harvested by March. Some vegetable gardens are located directly in front of villages, while others may be located several kilometers away. These gardens are of particular importance to women, who play a crucial role in caring for crops and managing the income generated from them.

The Mekong River and its many tributaries are the essence of the natural wealth and form the foundation of livelihood security and economies of local communities in the Mekong Basin. During the past decade, however, the Mekong has increasingly been disembedded from local fabrics of self-reliance and transformed into an exploitable economic resource for national and transnational production and development. Various countries have given a pre-eminent role to hydropower and irrigation projects, incorporating a cascade of electricity-generating dams along the Mekong and its tributaries. This trend towards technical and engineering works implies increasing state control over the management of the Mekong Basin. The absence of established public participation processes in the riparian countries also means that there is no level at which the public can effectively influence the planning, construction, or operation of most projects.

The planning and construction of hydroelectric dams and associated irrigation schemes on the Mekong is one of the most critical issues facing sustainable management of the Basin's natural resources. Hydropower projects have serious implications for fisheries and agriculture. Yet, governments of the Mekong Basin have paid very little attention to these implications. "Develop now, clean up later" is the paradigm of most leaders of Mekong countries, reflecting the mandate of governments to promote growth and expansion over local communities and healthy environments. As a result, the desirable objective of sustainable development—a balance between national growth and healthy local communities and environments—is far from being achieved.

In addition, there are conflicts between various stakeholders over multiple uses of water in the Mekong Basin, with very little awareness of the requirements necessary to maintain sufficient flows and a water quality that will sustain a functioning ecosystem. The conservation of river fauna and aquatic diversity in the Mekong is further constrained by problems intrinsic to freshwater habitats. Rivers are open, directional systems, and elements of the biota range widely, with aquatic animals using different parts of the habitat at various junctures in their lives. A particular problem of the giant catfish and many other fishes in the Mekong is that they migrate to different parts of the river during the breeding season. Such migratory patterns put fish at risk from stressors or human impacts in different parts of the river basin and at different times, and long-lived species may be highly vulnerable.

Because most species in a diverse fauna are rare, however, the tendency for environmental stress or habitat degradation and fragmentation to cause a reduction in the overall number of species is easier to predict than the actual identities of the affected species. Inadequate inventories and taxonomic knowledge exacerbates this information gap. For this reason, experts on freshwater biodiversity (Sheldon 1988, Dudgeon 2003) have proposed that conservation strategies should focus upon the entire fauna within a large drainage basin or eco-region rather than on management of rare species (Baran and Baird 2003). This approach makes sense in the context of large-scale hydropower developments in the basin where impacts on entire assemblages of species can be anticipated. However, even if we agree that conservation strategies operating at the scale of the drainage basin make sense, few mechanisms exist to facilitate conservation and management on this scale. Effective transnational organizations, such as the Mekong River Commission, are needed to deal with the challenge of sustainable management of complex ecosystems that extend over a host of countries with differences in socio-political contexts and policies towards the environment.

Although damaging to river ecosystems, to freshwater biodiversity and to local communities, the construction of dams and large-scale flow regulation schemes provides immediate benefits through generation of electricity and short-term relief from floods and droughts. Most benefits, especially cheap electricity and flood protection in low-lying areas, are felt some distance away in cities, while the negative impacts of dams are felt locally by rural riparian communities. The devastation of local fisheries caused by the construction of Pak Mun Dam on a Mekong tributary in northeast Thailand and the Nam Theun 2 Dam in Laos are just a few cases in point. This pattern of local impacts versus distant benefits causes conflicts between rural and urban dwellers. But since cities are centers of politico-administrative power, these conflicts tend to be settled in favor of the cities. It is thus not surprising that the detrimental effects of hydropower projects on biodiversity and local communities receive very little consideration when dams are planned in the Mekong region. The value of freshwater biodiversity has been overlooked, and the livelihoods of large numbers of local people have been, and continue to be, affected by the construction of megaprojects under the centralized control of states.

TWO

———

Transnational Enclosure

Over the past decades, the countries of the Mekong Basin have increasingly turned their interest to growth-oriented industrial development. As such, national policies have placed pre-eminent importance on hydropower and irrigation projects, spurring plans for a cascade of electricity-generating dams along the Mekong and its tributaries. This trend towards technical and engineering works implies increasing state control over the management of the Mekong Basin. The absence of an established public participation process in the riparian countries also means that there is no level at which the public can effectively influence the planning, construction, or operation of most large-scale, technology-and capital-intensive projects. Increasing state control over the management of the Mekong Basin has resulted in a large-scale appropriation of land for the construction of dams, loss of the most productive farmland and prime forestland, denial of local rights and local resource management systems, and widespread environmental impacts.

The development of hydropower is considered by the World Bank and other financial institutions as the driving force for basin development. Today, the negative impact of large-scale hydropower projects has become one of the most critical issues facing sustainable management of the basin's natural resources (IRN 1999, 5). In 1986, China began work on eight hydropower dams and two reservoirs in Yunnan. The first dam at Manwan (1500MW) was finished in 1995, and the second, at Dachaoshan (1260MW), was finished in 2003. Others, including the 2.7 billion U.S. dollar Xiaowan Dam (4200MW) and Nuozadu (5000MW) are currently under construction. As China embarks on a process of industrial expansionism, the Upper Mekong Basin in Yunnan is of crucial importance in providing an avenue for both raw materials from lower riparian countries and for providing China with access to new and expandable markets. The Mekong Basin is seen as not only providing a vital access way for the growing economic center of Kunming, but also a link between the Yangtze Basin to South Asia and the Indian subcontinent, which have enormous economic potential.

China has played an increasing important role in the Economic Quadrangle grouping of the Asian Development Bank. ADB initiatives are based on the rationale of fostering trade and economic growth as a means of strengthening subregional ties and cooperation. The Economic Quadrangle concept has led to the rapid expansion of infrastructural services, including construction of four highways linking Burma, Yunnan, Laos, and Thailand; and two railway projects one linking Yunnan, Laos, and Thailand, the other Yunnan and Vietnam. In addition to being the site of these new highway and railway projects, the Mekong is also recognized as crucial to subregional economic cooperation. Jinghong and Guanlei ports in Yunnan have been expanded to facilitate an increasing volume of trade between Yunnan, Chiang Saen, and Luang Prabang. The Mekong Commercial Navigational Agreement, which includes Yunnan, Burma, Laos, and Thailand, was signed in 2000. The aim of the Agreement is to blast away big boulders, shoals, and reefs in the mainstream of the Mekong to create a navigational waterway that can accommodate cargo ships of up to five hundred tons.

As Hirsch and Choeng (1996) observed, the salient objective of most infrastructure development projects is solely to facilitate and strengthen the growth and competitiveness of core industrial centers in the Mekong Basin, often at the expense of its rural peripheries. For China, the highways and waterway will provide important avenues for exporting commercial goods to Thailand, Laos, and South Asia via Burma. China is furthering its informal relationship with repressive and poverty ridden Burma, as well as expanding its sphere of influence into Laos. In turn, Burma accesses Yunnan for the export of logs and precious jewels such as jade. Even the opium trade provides a good, albeit illegal example of the extensive commercial networks that exist; there are less stringent controls and U.S. leverage in Yunnan than in Laos and Thailand. Yunnan's status as the most powerful regional player and the uppermost Mekong territory magnifies the implication of any resource development the Chinese province embarks upon. A unilateral approach to resource development, combined with the closed nature of information flows regarding China's hydropower and irrigation plans in Yunnan, does not facilitate a subregional cooperative approach to basin management. More importantly, the threat of earthquakes in Yunnan, with subsequent damage to large dams and the potential for downstream disasters, exemplifies China's neglect toward responsible downstream impact minimization. Co-riparian countries in the Lower Mekong Basin thus find themselves in a powerless position to negotiate with China.

Next to China, Thailand is arguably the second most powerful subregional player. Unlike other co-riparian nations, Thailand has already exhausted most of its easily accessible hydropower potential, making the remaining sites problematic and controversial. Of all the countries in the subregion, Thailand has the most developed community of NGOs and a relatively free press and media. Criticism of planned megaprojects, especially on environmental and social grounds, can be actively voiced in the public arena. In the late 1980s, the environmental movement and grassroots organizations in Thailand successfully resisted the planned Nam Choan Dam in Kanchanaburi province which would have destroyed a large area of healthy forest reserves. However, even in Thailand, active criticism and opposition to planned megaprojects can be risky. In rural areas, activists and leaders of local organizations are regularly harassed and threatened. In the early 1990s, leaders of the resistance movement against Pak Mun Dam were shot and wounded.

Thailand has a rapidly expanding economy and an increasing demand for energy. But planned megaprojects are usually controversial and face strong resistance from environmental groups, NGOs, and academics. Over the past decade, the Thai government has changed its strategy regarding dam and water projects. To minimize public criticism, the Thai government is working with Burma and Laos to plan a series of major water management schemes intended to increase Thailand's supply of water and electricity. Thailand has shown much interest in Burma's water resources. A number of dams have been proposed in Burma's Salween watershed and in border provinces to export power to Thailand. Human rights and environmental groups fear that the planned dam projects in Burma could have devastating impacts. Several planned reservoirs would flood prime forest reserves, wildlife sanctuaries, villages, and farmland on both sides of the border. A large number of local people, most of whom are marginalized ethnic minorities, would be evicted and relocated from the proposed areas. Many of the ethnic groups along the Thai-Burma border are already refugees who have fled their homes to escape war and persecution by the ruthless Burmese military. On the Thai side, the majority of these displaced people lack citizenship and land title documents, which means that they would be unable to claim their legal rights to compensation for relocation, loss of land, and other damages resulting from these proposed hydropower and irrigation projects.

In Laos too, several large dam projects are being planned to export power to Thailand. In fact, Laos is becoming a major regional exporter of hydropower. Over the past few years, export of power from the Nam Ngum Dam has contributed a large proportion of Laos's total export earnings. As such, hydropower export to Thailand is seen by the Lao government as a major source of revenue. Several plans for new dams are being proposed, most of them intended to produce power for export to Thailand. Independent of cooperation with Burma and Laos, Thailand has also proposed several plans for diverting water from the Mekong, the Mae Lamao, and other rivers in the north and northeast to feed the growing demands of Bangkok and the central areas of the country. When we revisited our research sites in March 2009, Mekong River water levels were well below normal, affecting both fishing and transportation of cargo. Chiang Khong and Chiang Saen were experiencing a severe drought due to the dramatic decrease of water level and the onset of earlier-than-usual summer heat. Sandbars and rocks were clearly visible resulting in cargo ships transporting goods between

China and Thailand facing navigational and docking difficulties at Chiang Saen. Ships have been forced to reduce their cargo by half to avoid running aground.

The Growth-Oriented Development Paradigm as Enclosure

The implications of large-scale hydropower development in the Mekong Basin are diverse and complex. While the potential economic returns are significant, the socioeconomic and environmental risks are also very high. The ecological and social consequences of hydropower development, such as the construction of a series of dams on the Mekong and its tributaries, are scarcely considered in the discourse of states and inter-state arenas. Despite the many negative and unintended consequences of megaprojects on the environment and local livelihoods, various governments inaugurate the process of privatization, decentralization, and clarification of property regimes in order to facilitate the process of market-based development.

Since the early 1960s, the growth-oriented development paradigm has served as a hegemonic discourse in which Thai rural populations have been objectified, ordered, and controlled. This development paradigm later spread to other countries in the Mekong Basin, especially Laos and Cambodia, at an increasing pace. Powerful forces of rural transformation and differentiation emerged through the extension and penetration of state agencies governing access to and control over resources, in turn linked to larger economic and political forces responsive to the interests of a dominant minority. Modern nation-states have been built by stripping power and control from local communities and creating structures of governance from which local people are excluded. Similarly, the market economy has been expanded primarily by enabling state and commercial interests to gain control over territories traditionally highly valued by peasants, transforming both land and people into expendable resources for exploitation. By enclosing forests, the state and private enterprise have torn communities out of the fabric of peasant subsistence. By providing local leaders with an outside power base, unaccountable to local people, they have undermined local checks and balances. By stimulating demand for consumer goods, they have impelled villagers to seek an ever wider range of goods to sell.

Only through the one dimensional growth-oriented development paradigm has it been possible to convert peasants into laborers within the global economy, replace traditional with modern agriculture, and free up the commons for the urban, industrial economy. Only by deliberately disassembling local cultures and reassembling them in new forms, has it been possible to open them up to global trade. To achieve the "condition of economic progress", millions have been thrown onto the human scrapheap as a calculated act of policy, their commons dismantled and degraded, their cultures denigrated and devalued and their self-worth reduced to their value as labor (*The Ecologist* 1993, 21–22).

Before the Thai economic miracle went awry in the late 1990s, for example, Thailand had enjoyed one of the highest rates of economic growth in the world. However, this growth had been concentrated mainly in the "private sector," namely, industry, commerce and banking, while other sectors, particularly agriculture, were left behind and marginalized. In other words, Thailand's outstanding business growth was achieved at the expense of other sectors, which contributed to a number of fundamental problems facing the nation. The first problem was that a high rate of growth was accompanied by destruction of the country's rich natural resources and rapid deterioration of the environment. Massive degradation of forests, agricultural land, and mangroves was combined with inequitable land ownership, increasing competition, and decreasing access to natural resources by local people. The second problem was the persistence of poverty among the marginalized rural majority, and the growing rural-urban income gap due to sectoral growth and structural change.

More importantly, the continuing degradation and depletion of the country's vital natural resources and the deteriorating environment due to unregulated industrial and urban growth led to growing competition and conflict over limited resources. This was simply because of the growing demand for land, water, and forests by non-agricultural sectors, and a growing and increasingly affluent and powerful private sector and urban population. Consequently, the very resources the rural poor depended upon to alleviate their poverty were taken from them.

If resource depletion, environmental degradation, poverty, and resource conflicts are allowed to persist, the sustainability of this growth will be undermined. Sustainability calls for the maintenance of the resource base and for the enhancement of both society's and nature's resilience. Yet advancing deforestation, a widening income gap, and growing resource competition and resulting conflicts serve to undermine the necessary resilience and stability of society and nature. Despite such grave problems, Thailand's impressive growth rate is cited by policy planners and technocrats as a conspicuous sign of the country's abundance, progress, and achievement. These people continue to entertain the false hope that the export-oriented economy and its resulting trickle-down effects would eventually benefit rural peasants, and that Thailand must continue to exploit its cheap labor and natural resources to serve as a better producer for the global market.

Why are an increasing proportion of Thai society being marginalized and why is the natural environment being rapidly and dangerously degraded? The answer is, in essence, that growth-oriented industrial development has been made possible through the rapid destruction of two of Thailand's most treasured traditional assets: a supportive local community and a healthy natural environment. In the neoclassical framework of growth-oriented development, community and nature are perceived as inessential features. People are reduced to labor, the environment to land, community and social institutions to the market, and economic success to growth in production. The result—in a world where the actual value and vulnerability of both community and the environment render the simplification well wide of the mark—is a development paradigm that is underdeveloped and counterproductive (Ekin 1990, viii).

In the pursuit of private sector profit maximization and growth, the entire state machinery has been transformed from the function of governing to that of business administration, accommodating changes or "structural adjustments" as dictated from the outside, aptly named international economic order. In this context, national governments of the Global South are transformed into "business machinery" whose functions are to facilitate the dominance of the private sector over other "inessential" sectors. This helps to explain why national governments in the Mekong region look to external forces such as the ADB for guidance in their business transactions, while increasingly turning a blind eye to their own people, particularly the overwhelming majority who fail to keep up with the winds of change. This is precisely how a two-pronged development policy has come about: liberalism towards the private sector in contrast to authoritarianism towards all other sectors.

It is no wonder that the state machinery has been a significant helping hand in facilitating convenient access to cheap labor and natural resources, as well as other infrastructural services. In the context of this so-called economic liberalism and free competition, we witness that in many countries in the Global South, the Mekong Basin included, economic activities are implemented through authoritarian means, with force and violence if necessary. In one large-scale resettlement project in the northeast of Thailand set up a decade ago, for instance, local people in 2,500 villages within National Reserved Forests were evicted from their homes to pave the way for eucalyptus plantations and paper pulp factories. This phenomenon helps explain why the loss of community and environmental degradation inevitably go hand in hand with sectoral prosperity.

Closely related to the role of the state machinery in facilitating sectoral growth is the true nature of the so-called "free-market." The neoclassical, growth-oriented development model assumes that the market is free and rational—that it organizes the production of goods and services in the best interests of society. Conventional economic theories and policies notwithstanding, we witness in many countries in the Global South the tendency of the market to erode the two key conditions for its own success: competitiveness, undermined by increasing corporate concentration and authoritarianism; and the containing moral context of community, destroyed by increasing poverty, landlessness, unrestrained consumption, and uncontrolled self-interest.

Thus within the context of environmental degradation, resource depletion, and the expansion of the market mechanism and consumerism, we also witness a growing disparity in income between urban and rural sectors, as well as landlessness, agricultural unemployment and under-employment, a rise in urban migration, contract farming, an increase in prostitution, human trafficking, labor exploitation, and finally, the rapid transformation of rural communities.

Transboundary Impacts of Subregional Development

In the Mekong countries, the expansion of the market economy has led to the transnational enclosure of the basin's resources, which means, in effect, that resource management systems are increasingly centralized. Increased centralization enables state and commercial interests to gain control of and transform territories traditionally used by local people into exploitable resources. Enclosure tears local peoples and their rivers, lands, forests, knowledge, and cosmologies out of the cultural framework in which they are embedded and forces them into a new framework which reflects the interests of the states and dominant groups. In this sense, the Mekong is dis-embedded from local fabrics of self-reliance and redefined as 'state property.' It is transformed into an exploitable economic resource and turned into a series of hydropower dams and waterways for commercial navigation and trade.

Enclosure transforms the Mekong into a "resource" for national and transnational production and development. Control over this resource is assigned to actors outside local communities. In the process of enclosure, societies are reorganized to meet the overriding demands of the market, ushering in a new political order. When the environment is turned over to new users, a new set of rules and new forms of organization are required. Enclosure redefines how the environment is managed, by whom, and for whose benefit. By enclosing the Mekong, states have torn it from local control. This breakdown of local control sets the course for the degradation of natural resources, with serious implications for local livelihoods.

Ecological change brought about by the construction of hydropower dams has wreaked havoc on thousands of fishing communities. The natural rhythm of water levels is closely tied to the migration of fish, a major source of income and protein for millions of people in communities along the Mekong and its tributaries. As of recent years local fishermen can no longer be certain of the Mekong's rise and fall. Water levels now change so rapidly and unpredictably that local fishermen can barely catch up. Their local knowledge and fishing gear are fast becoming obsolete. In the stretch of river between Thailand's Hat Khrai and Laos's Huai Xai villages, for instance, local fishermen have caught *pla buek*, the giant catfish, for decades. Here, a huge shoal divides the river, narrowing its channel. The riverbed is flat and composed of gravel, an ideal site for laying nets. After the completion of the Man Wan dam in Yunnan a decade ago, however, local fishermen in Hat Khrai began to notice unnatural variations in the flow of water. Since then, the catfish catch has gone down as the utility of fishing gear has diminished in light of the change in water levels. Many local fishermen can no longer fish and have had to find new livelihoods. In addition to unnatural variations in the flow of water, the blasting of shoals and reefs to expand commercial navigation on the Mekong has also had a considerable impact on local fishing communities.

As Campbell (2002, 101–2) points out, there are three potential areas of significant environmental impact from the commercial navigation project on the Mekong. The first is the impact on aquatic invertebrates and productivity within this stretch of the river. The removal of rapids and reefs or the deepening of shallow areas has significant implications for invertebrate diversity in the Mekong. The second is the impact on fish, especially migrators (Poulsen and Valbo-Jorgensen 2000, Sokheng et al. 2000). The Mekong River Basin is endowed with an immense diversity of aquatic fauna. The most well-documented study of aquatic fauna, fish, records no less than 1200 species. This diversity in turn creates the foundation for the livelihoods of millions of people living within the river basin (Vissler and Poulsen 2003, 22).

Disturbance to fish in any part of the basin, either through direct destruction of populations or through interference with reproductive or migratory activities, may have adverse effects at sites remote from those at which the disruptive activity takes place. Local populations of fish could be eliminated due to the blasting activities. But more importantly, long-term impacts could result from the channelization process. Migrators use the areas behind obstructions as resting places when they transit areas of fast currents. Removal of such obstructions may result in reduced migration success or, in extreme cases, totally block migration. If this were to occur for species of fish that are important to the livelihoods of local fishing communities, it could result in a significant impact on the poorer populations of the Mekong Basin.

The third potential impact of the commercial navigation project is on the terrestrial ecosystems of the basin. Opening the Mekong to larger barges and increased human traffic will bring poachers of timber and wildlife. Easier access to the area will increase the numbers and size of human settlements on the riverbanks. Coupled with the declining fish population resulting from blasting activities, this will eventually lead to a wide range of socioeconomic impacts. Local communities may be pressured to find new livelihood activities, including the expansion of hill farms with the clearing of more forest land, increasing timber harvesting, and wildlife trading.

One very important study of fish migrations in the Mekong River Basin, Poulsen and Viravong (2003) strongly supports the assumption made by other scholars that the Mekong is one of the richest freshwater biodiversity complexes in the world. The complexity and diversity of the Mekong ecosystem is represented by a variety of aquatic habitats, including mountainous streams and rivers with interchanging pools and rapids, slower flowing rivers in the lowland plains, lakes and swamps, waterfalls, and deep pools within mainstream rivers and tributaries. All these different habitats form unique ecosystems and are at the same time integrated parts of the Basin. These habitats or ecosystems interconnect to form a vast and complex aquatic network, which constitutes one single, gigantic ecosystem, the Mekong River Basin. In addition to the spatial dimension of ecosystem complexity, there is also an equally important temporal dimension. The annual southwest monsoon rain injects a seasonal "flood pulse" of water into the Mekong ecosystem, resulting in the overflowing of lakes, swamps, and riverbanks, and creating a vast area of seasonally inundated floodplain habitats. These seasonal habitats are rich in food, extremely productive, and account for the bulk of aquatic output in the basin.

The seasonal flood pulse is the driving force of the Mekong ecosystem. Many species of fishes have evolved life cycles that enable them to take advantage of these productive seasonal habitats. Their migratory and spawning habits are totally in tune with the monsoonal flood pulse. As Poulsen and Valbo-Jorgensen (2000) have shown, many Mekong fish spend the dry season literally fasting in deep pools and other refuge habitats within the main river channels. The arrival of the monsoon rain and its floodwaters is an ecological trigger for both migration and spawning. Spawning at the right place and time allows offspring to enter floodplain habitats rich in food and nutrients. Certain fish species spawn in the floodplain itself, while others migrate upstream to spawn within the river channel, leaving it up to the current to carry their offspring to the downstream floodplain habitats. In addition to the newborn offspring, many larger juveniles and fully grown fish actively migrate from dry-season refuges to floodplain habitats. The annual rhythms and life cycles of migrators connect the upstream spawning habitats and floodplain rearing habitats of rivers to form one interconnected and indivisible ecological unit of the Mekong Basin (Poulsen and Viravong 2003, 10). However, water-related development projects tend to block migration corridors, thus preventing this necessary shift between habitats.

Based on surveys of local knowledge, scholars have made general observations on the migratory patterns of fish in the Mekong River Basin. Poulsen and Viravong (2003) identify three main migration systems in the Mekong. The first migration system, the Lower Mekong Migration System, covers the stretch from Khone Falls down to the

Tonle Sap system in Cambodia and the Delta in Vietnam. This migration system is driven by the spatial and temporal separation of flood-season feeding and rearing habitats in the south, and dry-season refuge habitats in the north. The rise in water levels at the beginning of the monsoon season triggers the movement of many migrators from their dry season refuges in deep pools along the Kratie-Stung Treng stretch just below Khone Falls, towards fertile floodplain habitats in southern Cambodia and the Delta in Vietnam. Some species spawn in or around the floodplain, whereas others spawn far upstream and leave it up to the current to carry their offspring to downstream floodplain habitats. One of the key factors in the integrity of the Lower Mekong Migration System is the Tonle Sap, a vast and complex system of rivers, lakes, and floodplains. As a result of the natural increase in water discharged from the Mekong River at the onset of the monsoon season, the current of the Great Lake changes its direction, flowing from the Mekong into the Tonle Sap River and towards the Lake. The Lower Mekong Migration System contains the bulk of the Mekong fisheries.

The second migration system, the Middle Mekong Migration System, covers the stretch from just above Khone Falls upstream to Loei River in Thailand. This migration system is characterized by the presence of floodplain habitats associated with several large tributaries, particularly the Mun, Songkhram, Xe Bang Fai, and Hinboun rivers in Laos and Thailand. Fish seasonally migrate from mainstream dry season refuges to floodplain habitats via these tributaries. At the beginning of the flood season, the fish generally move upstream within the Mekong mainstream until they reach the mouth of one of these major tributaries. They then enter the tributary, from which they eventually gain access to their floodplain habitats. At the end of the rainy season, the movement goes in the opposite direction, from floodplains through the tributaries to the mainstream, where many fish spend the dry season in deep pools.

The third migration system, the Upper Mekong Migration System, covers the stretch from the mouth of Loei River in Thailand to the border between Laos and Yunnan. This migration system is characterized by a relative lack of floodplains and major tributaries. Nevertheless, it is also dominated by seasonal migration from dry-season refuges in the mainstream to spawning habitats further upstream. The most well-known member of this migration system is again the giant catfish. The Upper Mekong Migration System is also a multispecies migration system, although the total number of species may be lower than that of the other two migration systems.

The three migration systems briefly mentioned above are representative simplifications of the complex multispecies migration networks that crisscross and interlink the entire basin. It is highly important to note that these migration systems should not be viewed as "isolated" ecosystems, independent from each other. Although further research is needed before definite conclusions can be drawn, various scholars e.g. Roberts (1993), Roberts and Baird (1995), and Poulsen and Viravong (2003) have contended that the Mekong's migratory fish are transboundary stocks which extend beyond national borders. Conservation of migrating fishes thus requires management strategies at the basin level as well as at the local level.

Studies of the importance of flood timing to fish (Baran and Baird 2003, 82) clearly demonstrate that the migration of many important species of fish in the Mekong is triggered by a rise in water levels. Should this rise be delayed or reduced by dams, migration will be affected. The amplitude and timing of annual flooding are important determinants for the productivity of the river (Mattsen et al. 2003, 91). The availability and quality of inundated floodplains, in conjunction with hydrological factors, has a strong influence on total fish production. Therefore an integrated approach to water, water-dependent resources, and the natural environment is necessary to avoid unsound development options that would threaten food security basin-wide. At the national and subregional levels, however, this importance of water-dependent resources for livelihoods is yet to be recognized. (Baran and Baird 2003, 79).

In addition to fish and other aquatic resources, the cultivation of dry season riverbank vegetable gardens along the banks of the Mekong and many of its tributaries is a very important livelihood activity for local communities (Shoemaker, Baird and Baird 2001; Blake 2003). In many villages, produce from riverbank vegetable gardens is a major contribution to family food supplies. Riverbank vegetable gardening is a traditional, low external input farming system that has been practiced by the Tai, Lao, Khmer, and other lowland ethnic groups in the Mekong River Basin for at least a thousand years. From Yunnan down to the Delta region in Vietnam, riverbank vegetable gardens provide food and cash incomes for rural farming families.

The productivity of riverbank vegetable gardens depends on the annual flood-ebb cycle of the Mekong and its tributaries. Nutrient and sediment retention, groundwater recharge, flood control, flow regulation, erosion control, salinity control, water treatment, and ecosystem stability are but some of the more important functions of the Mekong wetland floodplains that we are just beginning to appreciate (Blake 2003, 107). During the four to six month period of riverbank flooding, the silt-rich water provides nutrient accumulation, kills off leftover vegetation and weeds, and provides pest control and groundwater recharge for the next agricultural season. In summary, the natural flooding cycle plays a vital role in regulating floodplains and maintaining the incredible productivity of wetland ecosystems.

As water levels fall, vegetable beds are re-dug, the shape and size of each bed determined by many factors including the slope of the bank, the types of crops to be planted, the amount of labor available and the land tenure of the farmer. Some beds may be raised, while on gentler inclines beds are not terraced at all and may run down or across the slope. The incredibly broad range of crops planted in riverbank gardens reflect local culinary preferences, risk minimization, and adaptation to market demands. It is quite common for a single family to plant several dozen different kinds of vegetables in one plot. A study on the lower reaches of the Songkhram and Mun rivers in northeast Thailand (Blake 2001) found at least forty-eight crops types grown in ten riverside communities surveyed. Riverbank vegetable gardens are "cultural land-scapes" (Yos 2003, 13–14) created by local management practices of growing, collecting and preserving plant genetic resources. The practice of planting and conserving a diversity of local cultivars is an important component of sustainable agricultural strategies to reduce pest damage and maintain yield stability.

There are two overlapping periods of riverbank gardening, both of which relate directly to the natural rise and fall of the Mekong and its tributaries. The first period of gardening is from August or September to December or January. Crops are planted in the moist, fertile soil of the riverbank as soon as the floodwaters begin to recede. Crops planted include long beans, mung beans, peanuts, yams, corn, cucumbers, cassava, chillies, pumpkins, eggplants, and many other varieties of local vegetables. In December or January, the second cultivation period begins. Additional crops are grown further down the riverbank as the water level continues to recede and a larger area of land can be cultivated. Crops planted during the second cultivation period include cash crops with short growing seasons such as lettuce, cabbage, Chinese parsley, and watermelons. In Laos, as Shoemaker, Baird, and Baird (2001) observe, tobacco grown in riverbank gardens is the single source of cash income for local villagers living along the Mekong River and its tributaries.

The riverbank vegetable garden is a traditional agro-ecosystem of great importance for villagers in poorer communities in the Mekong Basin. On the surface, the practice of riverbank gardening by local farmers seems unremarkable. But upon careful observation, it is clear that this traditional agricultural system is closely related to sustainable development, not only in terms of sustaining local livelihoods but also in terms of conserving local knowledge on biodiversity management, selection, and development of plant cultivars, and sustainable agriculture.

In recent years, however, the practice of riverbank gardening has declined, especially in the northeast of Thailand where out-migration of young people from the village has caused severe labor shortages. Direct loss of riverbank gardens resulting from large-scale development projects, especially dams and erosion control projects, has been documented in the case of Pak Mun Dam. In Laos and Cambodia, riverbank vegetable gardening is still relatively common, both along the mainstream

Mekong and its tributaries, providing vital nutrition and cash income to rural villagers. But in these countries too, the practice of riverbank gardening is increasingly threatened by massive hydroelectric, irrigation, and flood management schemes. The construction of additional mainstream dams in Yunnan could spell disaster for the future viability and productivity of riverbank gardens along the entire length of the Mekong. These dams will radically alter the hydrology of the Mekong, with greater dry season flows and diminished wet season flows anticipated. Greater dry season flows means that most traditional riverbank cropping areas would be inundated.

There is a need to critically evaluate proposed river development projects by Mekong governments with a long-term perspective, and with particular emphasis on transboundary impacts on biodiversity, ecology, and the livelihoods of rural riparian communities. As Blake (2004, 72) eloquently states, "the Mekong and its riparian communities are suffering the death of a thousand cuts to their life support mechanism", with transnational enclosure and the resulting unsustainable development gradually strangling the life-giving waters and natural hydrology of the Mekong River Basin.

PART II
MARGINAL COMMUNITIES, MARGINAL LIVES

THREE

Lue Villages on the Lancang

Manfeilong, a village of 346 inhabitants, is a Dai or Tai Lue village on the northern bank of the Lancang River. The Dai or Tai Lue are the lowlanders of Xishuangbanna Dai Autonomous Prefecture in southwestern Yunnan, and part of the larger Tai ethnic group in Southeast Asia which includes the Lao and Thai. Manfeilong, or Feilong village, is a typical Lue village where agriculture is the major means of production. It is located about thirty kilometers downstream from Jinghong, the capital of Xishuangbanna, which local Tai Lue residents refer to respectively as Chiang Rung and Sipsong Panna. Manfeilong borders the villages of Manda to the North, Mannao to the West, and Manfadai to the East. To the South, it faces Manlong on the southern bank of the Lancang River. Manfeilong falls within the administrative district of Manda, in Muang Han Township, and Muang Han straddles the southern frontier of Jinghong City.

Sipsong Panna was traditionally a major center of Tai Lue civilization. After the Communist Revolution, it was annexed by the Chinese government and absorbed into Yunnan Province, forming China's frontier with northwestern Burma and northern Laos. The land area in Sipsong Panna is comprised of lush forests and supports rich biodiversity, and 20 percent of its total of 19,690 square kilometers is classified as nature reserve. Approximately ten ethnic groups, including the Lue, Hani, Bulang, Lahu, Jinuo, Yao, Wai, Kuchong, and Khamu, make up a total population of over 840,000. As a frontier area with abundant biological and cultural diversity, the development strategy for Sipsong Panna is based upon agricultural production, with tourism being promoted as a rapidly growing industry. In recent years, Sipsong Panna has

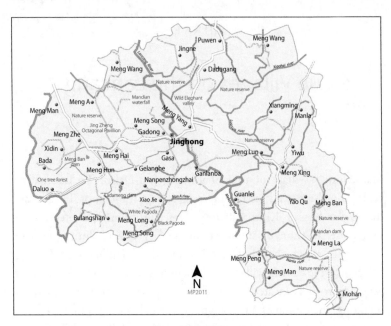

Map of Sipsong Panna

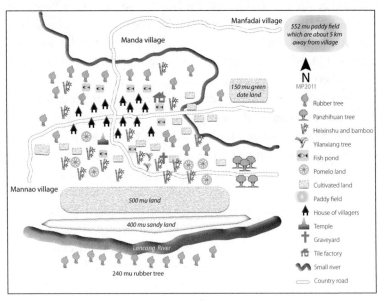

Map of Manfeilong

also become an important trading and service center between China and other Southeast Asian countries.

The Lancang, as the Mekong is known in China, flows across Sipsong Panna from northwest to southeast. Two major mountain ranges—the Nu and the Wuliang—extend from northern Yunnan through Sipsong Panna to Laos, occupying both sides of the Lancang. Elevation of the main basins, including Chiang Rung, Muang Han, Muang Jie, Muang Hun, Muang Hai, Muang Lai and Muang Pong, ranges between 500 and 1,100 meters, while mountain areas are from 1,000 to 2,300 meters above sea level. The ecological distinction between basins and mountainous areas has led to different modes of agricultural production and lifestyles of various ethnic groups. The Tai Lue, the traditional majority ethnic group, have maintained dominant status in politics, culture, economy, religion, and language for many centuries. Almost all the Lue reside in the river basins, as lowland rice cultivation is their major means of subsistence.

Manfeilong

The seventy-one homes in Manfeilong are located on a plateau about one kilometer from the Lancang. There is a large quantity of riverbank land in this area where villagers plant numerous varieties of vegetables and cash crops during the dry season. The hilly area two kilometers from Manfeilong is occupied by the Hani people. A small stream flows southwest through the villages of Feida and Feilong, then into the Lancang. Manfeilong is four kilometers from the town of Muang Han, and three kilometers from Dai Park, a famous tourist destination in Sipsong Panna. Muang Han itself is a key port on the Lancang, as well as an important Sipsong Panna tourist destination. The total area of Muang Han Township is 301.5 square kilometers, with 53 percent forest coverage. The average altitude of its lowland areas is 500 meters above sea level, the average temperature 22.7°C, the average annual rainfall 1,131 millimeters, and the climate, mild and wet. The land is fertile: apart from rice, rubber trees and subtropical fruit are the major domesticated plants in the area.

Traditional *Dai* house

Khamsing was born forty-seven years ago in Manfeilong. His house, as with most Lue homes, is raised on hardwood piles two meters above the ground to avoid dampness and floods. The floor and the walls are made of bamboo. A large open verandah in front of the living quarters is partially shaded by a hardwood roof. The interior is divided by bamboo walls into a living room and several bedrooms. The open space beneath the house serves as a workroom where farming tools are repaired, and a farm truck and motorcycles parked.

Like most Lue villages in Sipsong Panna, the layout of Manfeilong is nucleated: houses are built close together to form a compact settlement cluster. Manfeilong villagers typically surround their houses with herbs and fruit trees like coconut, mango, and plum. Glutinous rice is the staple diet. According to Khamsing's father, there is a saying, "Lue people do not eat cultivated vegetables." Rather, they prefer to collect wild vegetables. Approximately thirty species of wild vegetables are available in various seasons throughout the year. From the Lancang, women also collect *kai*, a kind of freshwater weed, and *dao*, a kind of algae. These wild vegetables are an important part of the daily diet. Gathering vegetables is normally done by daughters, mothers, and older family members in the evening after the day's farm work. When family members visit the market in Muang Han, they occasionally bring back pork and other groceries, but basic everyday dietary needs are met by gathering food from the Lancang and forest areas around the village.

As in most Lue villages on the Lancang, the people of Manfeilong depend on fish for daily protein. Villagers consume fish fresh or process it into fermented fish paste for long-term storage. In addition to fishing in the Lancang, villagers also collect shellfish from streams. Chicken and pork are occasionally consumed, but beef is usually only eaten during festivities and rituals, such as housewarmings and New Year.

Nonetheless, some villagers raise cows and buffaloes for meat, and deep-fried fermented cow skin is a typical delicacy. Villagers also hunt small animals such as birds, bats, and frogs.

Buddhism is deeply embedded in the culture, art, music, and architecture of the Lue, and also plays an important role in the social and cultural life of Lue villages. Buddhism is of great significance to Lue identity. Indeed, the predominant element of being Lue is to be Buddhist, and the Lue distinguish themselves from the surrounding Han, Hani, and Lisu by this one important factor. Buddhism also plays an important role in defining social norms and proper behavior. Goodness is judged by the extent to which one tries to observe Buddhist precepts.

Women collecting *dao* from shallow water

Picking wild vegetables in a home garden

A Buddhist temple can be found in almost every Lue village. The temple plays an important role in social life. During New Year and other important traditional festivals, villagers organize and perform rituals at the temple to ask for blessings for a good harvest and good fortune. They also invite monks to their houses to drive out evil spirits when family members get sick or during childbirth. Formerly, parents sent their sons to learn to read and write at the temple: as well as moral ethics being taught to the children, monks taught Lue and Pali language. Even today, every male should take the vow of monkhood for at least one Lent period before marrying and starting a family, in order to undergo the spiritual training necessary

Jai Ban shrine in Feilong Village

to be ready for life's responsibilities. But under the influence of Han culture and modern education, traditional values surrounding the monkhood have begun to change, leading to a scarcity of monks in Sipsong Panna. In recent years, it has become increasingly popular for Lue monks to travel to Thailand to attain further training in Buddhism.

From Khamsing's point of view, a village is a residential unit as well as a social unit. He believes Lue people have a strong sense of village life; for him, most Lue take pride in being a member of their village and are concerned about how other people regard their village.

Each village has a village spirit called *Jai Ban*, "the heart of the village." Whether there is an important festival or a new house being raised, villagers make a ritual offering to inform the village spirit. In so doing, villagers express their recognition of the importance of social obligations and a sense of collectiveness. For them, cooperation is the basic theme of social relationships in the village.

In everyday life, the people of Manfeilong cooperate in house building and in cleaning and maintaining their temple. At weddings and funerals, representatives from almost every household come to help. The most outstanding form of economic cooperation is the exchange of labor in farming. Every peasant household has its own social network who may be called upon to help others. Such labor exchange groups are not necessarily composed of relatives and neighbors, although it is a tendency for households that live close together to work together.

Village affairs are usually managed by *bozhan* or *boman*, that is, the village head, and a number of respected elders. The *bozhan* is elected by village members. Traditionally, he is a learned man who has served as a high level monk, is well versed in Buddhism, and has returned to secular life. The *bozhan* is responsible for organizing and managing village affairs, conducting village meetings, and coordinating all rituals and celebrations in the village.

Since agriculture is the basis of life in Lue villages, land is of utmost importance. It is certainly true that the villagers of Manfeilong are not quite sure where the village proper ends and where neighboring villages begin. Despite the vagaries of geography, however, each village is far more than a collection of households in close proximity. If its boundaries are ill defined, the temple and the spirit house serve to ritually unify it. Administratively too, each village is treated as a distinct unit and agricultural land is clearly demarcated.

Manfeilong is one of the earliest settled villages in the area. Khamsing's father, an old timer of Manfeilong, tells of a legend where, a long time ago, a piece of land by the Lancang River was given by the *chao phaendin*, the king or lord of the land, as dowry to his son-in-law. The son-in-law's relatives then settled in the area. Later, this new settlement was split into five villages. Then came a tragic time when the Lancang flooded. Following the flood, residents of one of the five villages moved to Burma, those of another migrated to Muang La, and residents of the remaining villages moved to higher ground further away from the Lancang. These three villages were later named Manfeilong, Manlong, and Manbing.

Three years after the Communist revolution of 1949, the Chinese government declared the liberation of Sipsong Panna. The titles and power of the *chao phaendin* and all aristocrats were abrogated. The Lue kingdom came to an end. In January 1953, Xishuangbanna Dai Autonomous Region was established, and the region was divided into twelve *panna* or *banna*. In 1955, the region was renamed the Dai Autonomous Prefecture, and in 1957, the twelve *banna* were redivided into five, each enjoying the status of a county. In 1959, the five *banna* were replaced by three counties, namely, Jinghong, Muang La, and Muang Hai. In 1994, Jinghong County became Jinghong municipality. Thus today the Xishuangbanna Dai Autonomous Prefecture has under its administration one municipality and two counties.

From 1953 to 1956, land reform was carried out in China. In ideal terms, the socialist transformation proposed by the Communist Party involved a transfer of economic ownership from private to public hands. Social classes were abolished, debts owed by peasants to the lords were forgiven, and private land was appropriated and redistributed to peasants. Small private enterprises and farms all over China were coerced to merge into cooperatives, to be managed and operated communally by members who distributed the profits among themselves.

In 1956, land reform arrived in Xishuangbanna. Each household in Manfeilong received an average of 16 to 17 *mu* of land (3.6 *mu* = 1 acre). A year later, collectivization of farm land, the prerequisite for socialist transformation, followed. At that time, Lue peasants, who had only recently received rice fields assigned by the government and became owners of land, were caught up in the national fervor for setting up mutual aid teams and cooperatives. In theory, land was still privately owned, but peasant households organized themselves into work teams for exchange of labor and other forms of collaboration. In practice, the land became collectively owned, with individual peasants contributing their land and labor as stock shares in the cooperatives, from which they received bonuses at the end of each year.

In 1958, a nationwide campaign to set up people's communes was aggressively promoted by the government. According to national policy, communes functioned as governmental organs and local organizations at the same time. Private ownership of land was abolished. Peasants' draft animals and farm tools were taken by force and became communal property to be managed by the communes. Communes became the most basic unit of production and decision-making. Public mess halls, referred to as "big rice pots," were set up in every commune.

At that time, Manfeilong, along with another sixteen villages, were consolidated into one commune and a big mess hall set up in Manshaojing. Every household contributed all their food to the mess hall, and everyone could eat there. In the first year, the villagers were adequately fed under the mess hall system, but from the end of 1958 to 1960 all of China was struck by a major famine. In 1958 and 1959, the residents of seventeen villages were forced to plant a total area of more than 2,000 *mu* in cotton. Cotton cultivation reduced the total area of rice paddies, which worsened the food shortage in the following years. Manfeilong villagers were humiliated when they had to borrow hill rice from their Hani neighbors. The desperate attempt to increase agricultural production under the national policy of *yi liang wei gang* or "taking grain as the key link" drove local people to clear a great deal of forest land in mountainous areas. From the 1960s, forest cover in Sipsong Panna decreased rapidly from 66 to 26 percent (Hsieh 1989, 220), culminating thereafter in increasing natural disasters such as floods and drought.

Lue peasants were apprehensive about the commune system from the very beginning. The formation of communes disrupted Manfeilong life far more than any previous reorganization campaign. While under the previous cooperative system land was distributed and the nature of local work organization changed, the new commune system penetrated deeply into personal life. Not only were they required to give up their newly acquired private plots, but they were also forced to give up a variety of private possessions. Farm animals such as buffaloes, pigs, and chickens had to be turned over to the production team. Lue peasants' labor was exploited in a way that was previously unthinkable. Not only were many people forced to migrate to work far from home, but those who remained had very little private time. A precipitous decline in grain production greatly exacerbated local resentment. The increase of land planted in cotton and other industrial crops, the reassignment of labor away from the agricultural sector, and a gradual unwillingness to work without appreciable material reward increased to a point in 1960 when the government was forced to initiate a series of measures to reduce peasant alienation.

Communes were abandoned and various levels of local government restored; cooperatives again became the basic unit of production. In 1965, Manfeilong was split into two cooperatives, each functioning as a relatively independent production unit. In August 1966, Mao unleashed the Red Guards to create a cultural revolution, doing battle with revisionism, destroying the remnants of the old, and establishing a new order. "People's communes" were revived, with two new grassroots units, the Brigade and the Production Team, added to the administrative system. Manfeilong was incorporated into a production team under the Ba Xiang Brigade, with production and distribution carried out under a principle of "ownership at three levels and calculation on the basis of production teams," which meant the production team was the basic unit of accounting and grain was distributed under an egalitarian policy of "basic rations plus work-point allowances." This form of management lasted until the end of the 1970s.

With all economic activities carried out collectively and distribution conducted on an egalitarian basis, peasant initiatives were greatly dampened. The development of rice farming was retarded so much so that the prefecture, previously known as the "granary of southern Yunnan," had to import 25,000 tons of grain annually in order to meet the basic needs of its people. From 1972 to 1974, Manfeilong also suffered outbreaks of insects for three consecutive years. This combination of natural disasters and poorly conceived policies led to a continuous shortage of food all over Sipsong Panna. The decade from 1966 to 1976 Manfeilong villagers remember as a time of acute social and economic crises.

When Deng Xiaoping assumed leadership of the Communist Party in the late 1970s, China began the far-reaching and systematic reforms that ultimately decentralized political power and changed the way the economy and society functioned. In the early 1980s, communes were abolished and replaced with a household farming system in which each family leased land from the state. In theory, all land belonged to the state, but in practice the government eventually permitted leases of fifty years or more. The leasing system provided an effective means of re-establishing the incentives of family farming without turning all land over to direct private ownership.

The household farming system is marked by three features. The first is the separation of land ownership from use-rights. This entails an even reallocation of land through contract to peasant households on the basis of the size of the family or the amount of labor available. Reallocation is conducted under the premise that although the land remains collectively owned, peasant households have the right to use the land as they wish. Peasants are not allowed to buy, sell, or use land for non-agriculture purposes, nor are they allowed to leave it to waste.

The second feature of the household farming system is the integration of collective farming with individual operation by peasant households. Under this system, peasants have the right to make land-use decisions according to their will, but they must submit to the guidance of the collective. Each household has the obligation to contribute labor to public works such as the building of roads and irrigation canals, which are organized by the collective. The third feature of the household farming system is that, taking into consideration the interests of the state, the collective, and the individual, it is required that one portion of the yields from leased land be handed over to the state as tax, one portion be sold to the state at a fixed price, and one portion be retained by the collective as public welfare. The remainder of the yields belongs to the individual peasant.

These politico-economic reforms produced spectacular growth in agricultural output and in peasant standards of living. In 1982, when the household farming system was implemented, there were some 60 households and about 600 *mu* of arable land in Manfeilong. After the reforms, with incentives for peasants the promotion of high yield rice led to a significant increase in harvested rice. In addition, the introduction of new farming machines enabled peasants to expand their farms and increase their income.

Manfeilong's economy today is clearly a local variation of China's national economy, which is essentially a capitalist market economy modified by state regulatory controls and centralization of natural resource management. On the surface, like most Tai Lue villages in Sipsong Panna, Manfeilong has grown considerably since the reforms of the late 1970s, however it still remains a peasant village that has capitalized on its traditional subsistence production. It is important to note that growth in the production system has not resulted in a breakdown of traditional subsistence production, but rather in its augmentation under the influence of the modern national economy. In 2004, there were 346 people in 71 households in Manfeilong, with 230 *mu* of gardens; 561 *mu* of rubber plantations, 552 *mu* of paddy fields, 45 *mu* of fish ponds, 150 *mu* of forest land, and about 1,100 *mu* of dry season riverbank gardens along the Lancang. With the exception of several young women who are employed in town, most villagers still engage in agriculture as their main livelihood strategy. Three shops and a tile factory in the village are run by outsiders.

Although Sipsong Panna has benefited a great deal from the booming tourist industry, the economic base of Manfeilong, as of most Lue villages on the Lancang, is still agriculture and fishery. However, an obvious trend over the past decade has been a decline in rice production and fisheries, and an increase in cash crop production. The main crops grown in Manfeilong today include rice, corn, pumpkins, white gourds, rubber trees, green dates, watermelons, and pomelos. Each Manfeilong household has an average of eight *mu* of paddy fields. As there is a need for glutinous rice in the Lue traditional diet and for religious activities, each household has one or two *mu* of paddy fields planted with glutinous rice, while the remainder are planted in high yielding hybrid non-glutinous rice. The heavy, late-maturing glutinous rice is primarily for household consumption. It is planted in May and June, and harvested in September and October. Glutinous rice yields 300 kilograms per *mu*, while hybrid rice yields 600 kilograms per *mu* and is sold at a price of 1.5 yuan per kilogram.

Corn is fast becoming a popular cash crop in Manfeilong. Due to the warm temperature, corn can be planted all year round. In 2002, a new variety of hybrid corn was introduced and later extended to a large area. In 2003, about 1,000 *mu* of land was planted with corn. Most households plant corn in November and harvest in March, but some plant in March and harvest in July. The average yield of corn is 500 kilograms per *mu*, and it is sold at a price of 1.2 *yuan* per kilogram. In 2004, Manfeilong villagers observed that their neighbors made a good profit from pumpkin. The following year, villagers planted about 200 *mu* of pumpkin. Pumpkin seedlings are planted in November, covered with a plastic sheet, and harvested in February. The average yield of pumpkin is 1,000 kilograms per *mu*, and it is sold at a price of 0.6 yuan per kilogram. Pumpkin shoots can be sold at a price of one yuan per kilogram. In 2005, Manfeilong villagers planted 200 *mu* of white gourd. The yield of white gourd is approximately 1,000 kilograms per *mu* and is sold at a price of 0.8 yuan per kilogram.

Manfeilong has 561 *mu* of rubber tree plantations, of which approximately 320 *mu* are located near the village. The other 240 *mu* of rubber trees are located on hillsides to the south of the Lancang. In 2005, nearly 500 *mu* of rubber trees could be tapped, and each *mu* generated an income of 2,500–3,000 yuan per year. March to November is the rubber season when trees are tapped once every two days. At this time of year, villagers get up very early in the morning to slash the rubber trees and return to collect the sap at noon. Rubber trees must be fertilized, and pesticides are used twice each year, in March and November.

Since the 1990s, watermelon has become a popular cash crop and several hundreds of *mu* are planted with watermelon each year in Manfeilong. The yield of watermelon is approximately 1–1.5 tons per *mu*, and is sold at a price of 0.5–1.5 yuan per kilogram. Three years ago, green dates were introduced to Manfeilong villagers. Green dates grow for twenty years, with a harvest season lasting from November to February of the next year. The yield of green dates is approximately 1–1.5 tons per *mu* and is sold at a price of 3–4 yuan per kilogram. All these cash crops require a great deal of chemical fertilizers and pesticides.

There are 552 *mu* of paddy fields in Manfeilong. The fields are located five kilometers away from the village, which is inconvenient for management. Since villagers have begun cultivating rubber trees and other cash crops, the importance of rice paddies in the village economy has declined markedly. Rice is now primarily grown for household consumption. Some households even rent out part of their paddy fields to outsiders at a price of 200 yuan per *mu*. Closer to the village proper, there was another 230 *mu* of paddy fields, but due to a shortage of water villagers converted these paddy fields into fruit orchards. Popular fruit trees include green date and pomelo, which were introduced to locals by Han Chinese merchants.

As the Lancang's water level decreases, riverbank land in Manfeilong is enlarged.

The large area planted in dry season riverbank gardens is an important source of income for Manfeilong villagers. As water levels fall during the period from October to July, vegetable beds are dug, the shape and size of each bed being determined by the amount of labor available and the land holdings of each farmer. There are approximately 1,100 *mu* of dry season riverbank garden land. From November to February, villagers plant a number of cash crops, including corn, pumpkins, and white gourds. These crops are planted in the moist, fertile soil of the riverbank as soon as the floodwaters begin to recede. After the pumpkins, white gourds, and eggplants are harvested, the second cultivation period begins. Crops planted during the second cultivation period include cash crops with short growing seasons such as lettuce, cabbage, Chinese parsley, and watermelons.

Manfeilong villagers earn extra income from fishing in the streams near the village and in the Lancang River.

Household Economy and Trade

The households of Manfeilong are well integrated into the market economy. On average, over 90 percent of total agricultural produce is sold, with only 10 percent retained for household consumption. Average household incomes vary little in Manfeilong, since farm sizes and agricultural production are rather similar for most households. Annual household cash incomes fall into the 55,000 to 60,000 yuan range.

Khamsing's family, for example, has five members: Khamsing, his father and mother, his wife, and one daughter. The family cultivates nine *mu* of paddy fields, six *mu* of orchards, ten *mu* of riverbank vegetable plots, ten *mu* of rubber tree plantations, and two *mu* of woodlands containing bamboo and firewood trees. In addition, Khamsing's family also has a one *mu* pond for fish farming and earns extra income from fishing in the streams near the village and in the Lancang. The following table shows the family resource and income generation pattern.

Table 3.1 Estimated Household Cash Income

Resource types	Land (mu)	Production time	Source of income	Income (yuan)
Hill farm	4	Whole year	Green dates	12,000
	2	Jan–March	Corn	800
		April–July	Corn	800
Riverside land	3	Dec–March	Watermelons	2,000
		July–Nov	Flooded (no income)	-
	4	Dec–March	White gourds	3,500
		April–July	Corn	1,600
		August–Nov	Flooded (no income)	-
	3	Nov–March	For rent	900
		April–July	Corn	1,200
		August–Nov	Flooded (no income)	-
Paddy	5	Whole year	For rent	3,000
	1	May–Sept	Glutinous rice	Family consumption
	3	May–Sept	Hybrid rice	Family consumption
Rubber plantation	10	Whole year	Rubber trees	30,000
Other	2	Whole year	Pomelos, peanuts, potatos, plums	2,000
Fisheries	Fish pond 1 mu	Whole year	Fish, snails, clams	1,000
	Fish in Lancang and small rivers	Whole year	Fish	2,000–3,000

Generally speaking, division of labor within the family is based upon gender and age. In the village, middle-aged married couples are mainly responsible for agricultural production, food gathering, and income generation for the family. They also manage important productive resources. For example, Khamsing and his wife manage the paddy land, orchards, and rubber plantation, while his elderly parents manage half a *mu* of vegetable gardens and the one *mu* fishpond. The division of labor within the family is so clear that even in busy seasons, Khamsing does not ask his parents for help. In many families in Manfeilong, members of the older generation build simple houses near fishponds or rubber plantations, and live apart from their married children. In addition to farming, Lue women are responsible for food gathering, cooking, cleaning, washing, and other household chores.

In recent years, a number of Manfeilong villagers have begun to rent out parts of their agricultural land to Han traders who use it to plant chili, watermelon and eggplant. Renting land to outsiders provides employment opportunities for both elderly women and young women in the village who are hired to look after the gardens at a minimum rate of 20 yuan per day.

Agricultural produce is sold at the nearby Ganlanba market. Occasionally, Han traders come to the village to purchase watermelons, white gourds, corn, and green dates. Although it is convenient for Lue peasants to sell their agricultural produce to small traders, the price they receive is invariably lower than at the local market. Khamsing's wife, like most Lue women, plays a leading role in negotiating the price of produce, and in managing the income and household expenditures.

Over the past decade, Khamsing has witnessed considerable changes in Manfeilong. The market economy is beginning to pervade the fabric of social life in the village. The increasing demand for agricultural produce to feed the growing numbers of tourists in Sipsong Panna and urban populations in China has brought about additional demands and a sharp increase in the price of farm produce, which is a great incentive to production. More and more cash crops are produced directly for the market. The entire process of agricultural production has come under the influence of the market and agricultural productivity has increased tremendously. Increasing productivity has also raised the income of Lue villagers, and is beginning to bring about a sharp increase in consumer spending.

The village economy has undergone a profound transformation. The demand for electrical appliances and other consumer goods has skyrocketed. The construction of new roads has allowed many convenient and novel commodities to flow in. Most Lue peasant households now own a small motorized farm truck, which serves as a means to transport agricultural produce from the village to Ganlanba market in Muang Han. All kinds of manufactured goods, from soap to motorcycles, have become daily necessities. In Manfeilong, some families have two to three motorcycles, and family members now ride motorcycles to their farms. These changes in consumption patterns mean that most peasant households find themselves in a situation in which more and more cash must be earned and spent to meet the needs of everyday life.

Changing Ecosystems and Local Resource Management

For more than a thousand years, Sipsong Panna has been the home of many ethnic groups proven to be knowledgeable natural resource managers. Lue villages are usually situated on flat land at the foot of mountains under canopies of mixed deciduous forests that form watersheds feeding small streams, which in turn feed into community production systems. Wet rice cultivation in the valleys and highland farming in the uplands makes the control and management of water crucial for local agriculture. Watershed forest preservation to ensure an abundant water supply has thus become an integral part of Lue cultural traditions and production practices.

Drought, delayed rainfall, and shortage of water are important factors that have forced local villagers to realize the imminent calamities of environmental degradation. Through their life experience, Lue people fully understand that if there was no forest, there would be no water source; if there was no water source, there would be no irrigated fields; if there were no irrigated fields, there would be no rice. Knowledge and wisdom regarding local ecology is developed through everyday experience. A harmonious coexistence between human livelihoods and the environment has emerged by virtue of tradition, manifested in beliefs that promote the preservation of forests and encourage cooperation in protecting the environment. Beliefs in sacred entities who roam the forests provide a basis for the use of forests and water in a humble and reverent manner, with deep consciousness of the sanctity of the forest and the sacred beings that inhabit it.

The importance of watershed forests has given rise to the Lue belief in *Long* forests. *Long* forests, usually located in the hills behind villages, are inhabited by ancestral spirits. Animals, plants, and water resources are thus considered holy and inviolable. Felling timber, gathering food, hunting or cultivation in *long* forests is forbidden. Religious beliefs and rituals not only provide a sense of security amidst the uncertainty of agricultural production, but also lay down a moral framework within which equitable distribution of resources is guaranteed. This moral framework of production and resource management is expressed in terms of local customs, taboos, and prohibitions against trespassing and overexploiting common property resources. Lue villagers believe that a person who violates these taboos will suffer misfortune or even sickness. Local communities propitiate the village and *muang* ancestor spirits annually to express gratitude for protecting watershed forests and providing water for production systems. Such beliefs have developed and crystallized to form the basis of moral power over resource management, and are thus closely related to agricultural production and food security.

In practice, *long* forests are a key link in the intricate connections between watershed forests, graveyard forests, temple forests, firewood and bamboo forests, irrigation systems, fish ponds, and paddy fields. Traditionally, Lue people would never have felled timber, cultivated crops or hunted in a *long* forest. Religious beliefs acted as effective means of forest conservation. Sipsong Panna is made up of approximately 30 *muang*s of various sizes and over 600 Lue villages. Each *muang* has a *long* forest which is home to the *muang* spirit, and each village also has a *long* forest in which the village spirit resides. Before 1958, there were over 1,000 *long* forests in Sipsong Panna, with a total area of 100,000 hectares, accounting for 5 percent of the total land area. These natural forests made a significant contribution to environmental protection, particularly in soil, water, and biodiversity conservation.

Along with *long* forests, graveyard forests are another form of local forest conservation and management. The graveyard forest is typically located one or two kilometers away from the village. Each village has a particular area that is designated as a graveyard forest. Outsiders are not allowed to enter, and no one is allowed to fell timber or hunt in the area. In every Lue village, the temple forest is yet another important form of forest conservation and management. In addition to being a place of worship, Buddhist temple grounds contain lush forests, where no one is allowed to disturb even a blade of grass. Today, the biggest tree in Manfeilong, rising thirty or forty meters in height, is the banyan tree in the temple forest.

Firewood and bamboo forests are usually located near the village for convenient management and transport. In this type of forest area, *heixinshu,* or Siamese cassia, is grown for firewood and bamboo for making utensils and for building. These plants are very important in the Lue people's lives. Every three years, the branches of Siamese cassia are cut as firewood and, if properly trimmed, more branches will grow. One family requires twenty Siamese cassia to ensure sufficient firewood. Bamboo has a variety of uses including for building houses, bridges, and bamboo rafts; and to make tables, stools, and traps to catch fish and birds. Bamboo shoots are also considered a delicious part of the Lue diet. Nearly every Lue household, then, plants a certain amount of bamboo. In Manfeilong, there are over ten kinds. Nonetheless, in recent years firewood and bamboo forest areas have been reduced. Villagers increasingly use timber and concrete to build houses; they also depend less on firewood than before.

Lue peasants usually designate forest areas on the mountain slopes surrounding villages as utility forests where hardwood trees for house building are planted. Next to the utility forests are home gardens where herbs and fruit trees such as coconut, mango, pineapple, and plum are planted. Vegetable gardens, paddy fields and fish ponds are located in the flat, low-lying areas. This terraced formation, with *long* forests at the highest elevation and paddy fields at the lowest, is typical of Lue human-ecosystem relationships.

The reproduction of traditional customs and practices related to forest management attests to the potential of local communities to put their local knowledge and deep understanding of natural resources to practical use. Lue people have a broad knowledge and holistic understanding of their environment, including species recognition and management of biodiversity and genetics. Local people and their forests have survived intact because, throughout history, the forests have provided people with the means of life, and in return, local people have practiced sustainable environmental management based on their knowledge and customs.

Bamboo is planted throughout forest and village areas.

Thus in 1953, the total forest cover in Sipsong Panna was over 60 percent. From 1958 to 1984, however, the traditional community-based natural resource management system gave way to an increasingly centralized one that was based on government initiatives. Natural resources declined rapidly as a result of the deliberate destruction of forests. This destruction was due to several factors. During the nation-wide fever for increasing production of steel, iron, and copper brought about by the 1958 Great Leap Forward campaign, a tremendous amount of trees were cut to fuel village furnaces. Meanwhile, the "doing away with superstition" campaign that started in the late 50s and lasted through the Cultural Revolution destroyed to varying degrees the *longshans* (dragon hills) of every village. Finally, the erroneous policy of "taking grain as the key link" resulted in the large-scale destruction of natural forests. By 1980, these factors combined reduced the percentage of forest cover in Sipsong Panna to a low 29.77 per cent.

In 1982, forest land in China was reclassified into three categories: state forest, collective forest, and household forest. State forests are managed by the Forestry Department; collective forests are managed by local governments, and the remaining forest land is contracted to individual peasant households as "responsibility hill land." The individual hill land policy entailed applying the household farming management system to the management of forest land. This was done without considering the significant difference between the output from forestry activities and that from agriculture. Forest products are generally slow to grow or generate any substantial benefits, and are not immediately related to daily necessities, differing vastly from agricultural products which can be sown and harvested within a one-year period. For this reason, peasants tended to take great care of their contracted farm land, while adopting a reckless attitude towards forest land contracted to them. While hill people often converted their contracted forest land to cultivated land, the Lue people in the valleys convert their contracted forest land to rubber or pineapple farms. This contract responsibility system in the management of forest resources did not in any way help to protect forests. On the contrary, it gave rise to a new surge of deforestation.

Since 1985, China has put into effect a series of laws and regulations for the protection of forest resources. The management of forest resources has become more and more centralized. Sipsong Panna prefecture has also adopted a series of measures to reinforce centralized management, including the establishment of five national nature preserves in areas where forests are relatively intact, with a total area of 3,600,000 *mu*. The launch of a large-scale tree planting campaign in June of each year, along with the adoption of preferential policies towards ethnic minorities in highland areas—reduction of grain taxes, the building of small-scale water conservation projects, introduction of irrigated rice farming, a sedentarization program to support permanent agricultural production on fixed settlements and reduce swidden land areas—are just a few examples of ineffective government measures to reduce forest degradation.

Over the past several decades, particularly since the Cultural Revolution, community-based resource management systems have been overlooked. Lue people's religious beliefs have been dismissed as fetishism and undermined. Overheated development resulting from the rush to industrialize has led to an insatiable need for timber and firewood. Consequently, a great number of *long* forests have been degraded or destroyed. Before the Cultural Revolution, there was over twenty *mu* of *long* forestland in Manfeilong, where large trees one to two meters in diameter could be found. In the 1950s, officers from people's communes came to fell the big trees in the *long* forests and carried them away. Their status as part of the *long* forests afforded these trees no protection. Afterwards, forest land was turned into agricultural land by villagers in Manfeilong themselves. Today, the younger generation in the village understands very little about the cultural tradition of conserving *long* forests.

Prior to the 1950s, there was little demand for timber in Manfeilong, since houses were primarily built of bamboo. Firewood was mainly derived from Siamese cassia. As a result, the village was surrounded by thick forests. Over the past several decades, Manfeilong's forest land has suffered waves of intrusion. In the early 1950s, workers from a nearby military camp came to the village and felled timber. In 1958, Hani highlanders came to the village to cut trees and clear new farmland. The Hani highlanders planted 150 *mu* of rice fields on Manfeilong forest land. Due to a lack of water, however, production was low, so in 1968 the Hani highlanders abandoned the land and left it to the Manfeilong villagers. The Lue now plant green dates on this land. Another wave of intrusion began in the sixties when villagers in Manfeilong and neighboring villages started to build houses with tile roofs. This new development led to an intensive demand for tiles, and a tile factory was set up in Manfeilong. Even though the quality of the tile was not good, the need for wood fuel to fire the kilns destroyed large areas of forest. Towards the end of the 1960s, the state began to promote rubber plantations. so villagers planted several hundred rubber trees around the Manfeilong. In the 1970s, an additional fifty *mu* of rubber trees were planted on the hills along the Lancang.

In the 1980s, when the household production system was first implemented, all forest land around the village and on the hillsides was allocated to individual households. Since it was deemed profitable to plant rubber trees, all households cleared their allocated forest land and planted it with rubber trees. Han outsiders came again to the village to buy the big *paizhihua* trees, many two to three meters in diameter, that were being felled. Suddenly, Manfeilong village lost two to three hundred *mu* of forest land along the Lancang to erosion. In Khamsing's opinion, this was caused by hydropower dams upstream.

Over the past several decades, forestland in this corner of Yunnan has gradually been degraded. The Chinese government has expanded its domain of power and control over natural resources in frontier areas. The introduction of a modern education system has contributed to a growing generation gap. Children of newer generations are growing up with consumeristic and materialistic values. Members of the older generations are looked down upon as illiterate and underdeveloped, their beliefs dismissed as backward and primitive. The modern education system is conducive to capitalist expansionism, and at the same time destroys the traditional values and local knowledge that have been passed down through the ages.

The expansion of the market mechanism into rural areas, particularly the expansion of commercial cash crops, has been an important factor affecting production and management systems of Lue villages along the Lancang. The enlargement of cultivation areas, together with the expansion of rubber plantations, invariably leads to monocultural production and forest degradation. Increasing use of chemical fertilizers and pesticides leads to soil erosion and water contamination. The construction of massive dams and hydro-electric power plants not only leads to further deforestation and a loss of biodiversity through the destructive use of natural resources, but also triggers rapid changes in the ecosystem and the rhythm of water flows. Water flows change so rapidly and unpredictably that local fishermen on the Lancang can barely adjust. Their local knowledge and fishing gear are fast becoming obsolete. In addition to the unnatural flow of water, blasting of shoals and reefs to expand commercial navigation on the Lancang has also had a significant impact on local communities.

Tourism, Dams and Rural Communities on the Lancang

Tourism has also become a fundamental industry in Sipsong Panna and a major catalyst of change. Dai Park in Muang Han, which attracts 600,000–700,000 tourists per year, has become a key tourist destination in Sipsong Panna. In order to strengthen and incorporate this local tourist destination into the international tourist route, the Xishuang-banna government is planning on building a highway connecting Muang Han and Muang Lun—another tourist attraction in Sipsong Panna where the biggest tropical botanic garden in China is located. When this project is completed, Muang Han will become a part of the ring road that connects to the Kunming-Bangkok highway. The local government is also planning to expand Dai park. According to this plan, the three riparian villages of Mannao, Manfeilong, and Manfadai will be incorporated into the enlarged Dai Park.

To protect the scenic resources on the banks of the Lancang in Muang Han for tourism, big trees such as *panzhihua, yilanxiang,* and even the big *henxinshu* that grow in local villages have been inventoried and reclassified as state property. Local villagers are displeased with this forced conservation, since they insist that all trees were allocated to villagers when the household production system was implemented in 1982. These trees should be considered household property, but under the new form of classification, villagers cannot fell the trees or make use of the timber. To counter this move, some villagers have been rushing to fell the big trees and sell the timber to traders. Even the *henxinshu* are being sold, roots and all; the traditional belief in *long* forests is fast being replaced by ineffective centralized regulations.

To further promote tourism along the Lancang, the local government is planning to build a scenic road along the Lancang from Muang Han to Manfadai. When the project is completed, riparian villages will have lost a large portion of their riverbank gardens. The wetlands alongside the Lancang, vital to the livelihoods of local fishermen, will also be destroyed. Although tourism may bring additional income to some Manfeilong villagers, the majority are not pleased with the project, since they stand to lose significant land resources, but it is difficult for them to make their voices heard within a top-down decision-making structure.

In addition to tourism promotion schemes, the construction of hydropower dams on the Lancang has also had a great deal of impact on local communities. Jinghong Dam is located about five kilometers north of Jinghong City. It is the sixth of a cascade of eight dams on the Lancang, with an installed capacity of 1,500 MW. The dam will be 118 meters high, with a common water level of 602 meters above sea level. The reservoir is 97.8 kilometers long and total reservoir storage is 1.04 billion cubic meters. Jinghong Dam is being built to allow the passage of 300 ton cargo ships. It is reported that 80 per cent of electricity generated will be exported to Thailand. The dam is scheduled to be completed in 2009 when it will submerge 2,575 hectares of land, including 1,210 hectares of nature reserve areas. Four counties will be affected, and over 2,000 people relocated.

The 150 MW Ganlanba Dam is scheduled to be built 25 kilometers downstream of the Jinghong Dam. The Huaneng Group, which is responsible for the construction of the Ganlanba Dam, claims that the dam is a component of the Jinghong Dam complex. It will serve not only to increase electricity generation, but also to improve navigation between Jinghong city and Muang Han.

Over the past decade, Lue villagers on the Lancang have been increasingly concerned about the impacts of dam construction on the local environment. Manfeilong villagers cannot help but notice that the

shoreline of the Lancang has changed a lot since 1995. That year, the sudden release of water from the Manwan Dam caused unprecedented floods which destroyed sections of the riverbanks. Since then, the river has receded and the water level has decreased considerably.

Sandy land along the shores of the Lancang

Khamsing points to the Lancang, saying:

"Just a few hundred meters from the riverbank, there used to be a small island in the middle of the river. In the rainy season, the island was submerged. In the dry season, we Manfeilong villagers would paddle our boats to the island and prepare the land for planting watermelon. But today, the river has receded so much that the island is now connected to the riverbank."

Beginning in 1998, the water level decreased several meters, and has never since reached previous levels. Large areas of sandy land have appeared along the shore. Four neighboring villages (Manfeilong, Manting, Mannao, and Manfadai) have cooperated to construct several small dikes to expand the riverbank land. As a result, riverbank garden areas have been enlarged, and an additional 4,000 *mu* of sandy land can be used for agriculture for a longer period of time. Some riverside land on higher ground can be utilized all year round.

Manfeilong alone has gained about 1,000 *mu* of riverbank land. During the first few years, the newly available land enabled every household to earn additional income from their enlarged riverbank vegetable gardens. In recent years, villagers can plant watermelons, pumpkins, and peanuts in their riverbank gardens from November to April when the water level is at its lowest. The rainy season starts in May, and in July the water level begins to rise gradually. At this time of the year, villagers usually plant maize on higher ground. In this way Lue villagers have adapted their agricultural production to accommodate the changing environment with a degree of success. However, villagers also recognize that the water level often changes unpredictably. For example, in June of 2004 the water level suddenly rose. Within three hours, the water submerged about 100 meters of riverbank, and 1,000 *mu* of land was inundated. A lot of villagers lost their crops. In recent years, the water level has become very low in the dry season. In April, villagers can walk across the Lancang. Fishing boats often become stranded on the shore. Villagers think this is mainly because upstream dams reserve water for hydropower, and there is little rainfall in the Lancang Basin.

Villagers can now walk across the Lancang in the dry season.

Of all the victims of development, fishermen are the hardest hit. Having lived in Manfeilong his entire life, sixty-seven-year-old fisherman Saeng said that although he never earns more than 20,000 yuan a year, he does not consider himself poor because he can get all the food his family needs from the river. According to Saeng, there are over forty species of fish in this part of the Lancang. Among them, about thirty species are of economic value. Saeng and several other older fishermen in the village reminisced about the good old days. "Twenty years ago, when we only had some paddy fields and no rubber trees or hill farms, nearly every family caught fish for food and income. The older men, in particular, spent their rainy days catching fish in the Lancang."

There are three main fishing grounds near Manfeilong. One is on a small tributary of the Lancang. Since the river is near the village, there are plenty of fish and the shallow water is not as dangerous as the deep water of the Lancang, so it is a good place for fishing. Over ten species of fish can be found here. Fish that can be found all year round include *bagang, bazhuan, bana*, and *badian*. When the rainy season comes, big fish such as *baha* and *bahei* enter the tributary from the Lancang River and can be caught. Besides fish, shrimp, snails, and clams can also be caught in the river. The gear mainly used for catching big fish are *hang* (bamboo fences that are placed across the stream), fish hooks, and bamboo traps. In the dry season, a person can catch an average of about five kilograms of fish from the river each day, while in the rainy season, a person can catch an average of about ten kilograms. Sometimes villagers can catch big fish weighing about ten kilograms by using a *hang* or a hook.

The second fishing ground is in a shallow area by the riverside. It serves as a habitat for many aquatic plants and animals. The area is an ideal place to find fish, shrimp, *hiuo*, a kind of small edible insect; *dao*, freshwater algae; and it is also a good place to raise ducks. About twenty species of fish can be found in the area, most of them small fish such as *bagong, bamo, babu, badian, bashadai, bahongwo, bamiti, babileng,* and *bamahao.* One common kind of fishing gear used in the area is small dredge nets with covers made of bamboo. A person can catch about one

kilogram of small fish and one to two kilograms of shrimp and *hiuo* here. Small fish are consumed by household members or used as bait to catch bigger fish. Shrimp and *hiou* can be made into popular dishes or sold to restaurants at a price of eight to ten yuan per kilogram. Since the water in this area is

Small dredge net to catch small fish

Hang

not deep, it is an ideal place for women and children to catch fish and collect *dao* for daily household consumption.

Manfeilong's third fishing location is in the Lancang. The rainy season, from May to October, is the best season to catch fish in the Lancang, since the water level is higher and there are many big fish. In the rainy season, local fishermen catch big fish such as: *bahao, bahei, bayang,* and *banai*, which can weigh as much as ten kilograms each, and medium size fish such as *bazalang, bamahao, bazang, baxilie,* and *bazhuan*, which can weigh over one kilogram each. Smaller fish such as *bamie* and *baha* are only found early in the rainy season. In the past, the main kinds of fishing gear used in the Lancang were hand nets, mainly used in open water and deep areas; *jiang*, a kind of net mainly used in shallow areas; and bamboo fish traps, used in open water. In the rainy season a person can catch about ten kilograms of fish per day. Certain fish such as *bahao, bazhalang,* and *bayang* have a high economic value and can be sold for 30 to 40 yuan per kilogram at the local market. Other types of fish can be sold at a price of 8 to 10 yuan per kilogram. A local fisherman can earn 5,000 to 6,000 yuan a year from fishing.

Manfeilong fishermen have noticed that their fish catch has declined over the past decade. Although there is no obvious change in the species of the fish, the amount of fish has declined by half. In the past, from the months of February to April when the *bazang* appeared, fishermen could catch six to seven kilograms a day. Now, however, after a hard day's work, they can bring home only one to two kilograms. Another example of the drastic reduction in the quantity of fish in the Lancang is *bazalang*. Schools of bazalang can typically be found in June. Local fishermen use hand nets to catch them. Several years ago, one netting could bring in one to two kilograms of *bazalang*, but now, to catch the same amount requires working hard all day.

Fewer and fewer fishing boats can be found in Manfeilong village these days, and the local fisherman's livelihood and culture will soon disappear if this situation continues. Saeng and his colleagues believe that the construction of several dams on the Lancang has caused unnatural changes in the water level. Changes have resulted in a reduction in the amount of fish and other food sources in the Lancang, and the utility of traditional fishing gear has diminished in light of generally reduced water levels. Saeng says that his fishing gear is now less effective given the changes in the river's ecology. In recent years, he adds, outsiders have begun to use big boats and large nets in the area to catch fish for commercial purposes. Sometimes these outsiders even use electricity and poison to catch fish.

As it has become harder to catch fish, traditional fishing gear such as hand nets and *jiang* are being replaced by draw nets and electricity, which causes further declines in fish. Such new fishing methods cause further degradation of the Lancang's resources.

Fishing boats on the Lancang

Although the local government has outlawed destructive fishing methods, they have been adopted by local young men on a small scale.

The amount of native fish in the small river near the village has also declined in recent years. Saeng's wife, Lah, complains that it has become exceedingly difficult to find fish in the river. "You're lucky

Fish caught in the Lancang during the dry season

to catch one kilogram of small fish," she says. "The snails, clams, and frogs found in the small river are also much smaller now, and don't taste as delicious as before." Lah believes that the river is now polluted because in 1995 a rubber processing factory was built upstream. Every year large amounts of waste water are discharged into the river.

Ever since the water level has gone down and the island in the middle of the river has merged with the riverbank, the wetland area along the Lancang has disappeared. Local fishermen have lost an important fishing ground. Wetlands now only emerge temporarily during the months of October and November. During these months, fishermen catch *luofei* and other small fish. Shrimp, *hiou*, and other food sources have also disappeared. Given this situation, fishermen are forced to change their way of life from wetland fishing to sandy land agriculture.

Saeng has a few final words:

"The Lue people in this area have made a living from the Lancang for hundreds of years. The decline in fish stocks has resulted in pressure on us fishermen to change our way of life. When the Jinghong and the Ganlanba hydropower dams and channelization for navigation starts, water levels will further fluctuate. Heavy commercial shipping will drive the last nail into the fishermen's coffin."

The Lancang fishermen's livelihood and culture will soon disappear if this situation continues, and the Lancang will no longer be a river of life.

FOUR

———

Riparian Communities
in Northern Laos

Lao PDR has few options for driving economic growth other than its potential to exploit timber and export hydropower.... (World Bank 1997, in IRN 1999: 5)

In most rural parts of the lowland plains of Laos, as well as in much of the uplands, fish and other aquatic animals provide between seventy and ninety percent of the animal protein in people's diet. For many of these people, not yet or barely in the cash economy, there is no affordable substitute source of protein. (Claridge 1996, in Bush 2003, 21)

The importance of natural resources to the people and economy of Laos cannot be overstated. Nearly 90 percent of Laos' total land area of 236,800 square kilometers is in the Mekong Basin. Approximately three-quarters of the total terrain of Laos is mountainous or hilly, with several large plateaus, and the land drains into the Mekong by more than a dozen large tributaries. About one-third of all water in the Mekong originates from watersheds in Laos, which in turn form a quarter of the total watershed area of the Mekong Basin. The country has one of the most extensive tracts of forest remaining in the Mekong Basin. According to the World Bank, Laos "has few options for driving economic growth other than its potential to exploit timber and export hydropower."

Laos's endowment of an abundance of water is complemented with extensive productive inland fisheries, upon which the majority of local people depend for their daily sustenance. Any watershed development project in Laos, whether on the mainstream of the Mekong River or its tributaries, thus has the potential to affect rural communities in Laos as well as in downstream riparian countries. In most rural parts of the lowland plains of Laos, as well as in much of the uplands, fish and other aquatic animals provide between seventy and ninety percent of the animal protein in people's diet. For many of these people, not yet or barely in the cash economy, there is no affordable substitute source of protein".

Laos has a population of approximately five million people, half of which are ethnic Lao, while the rest belong to one of over fifty ethnic minority groups. The overwhelming majority of the population is rural, residing in approximately 12,000 villages scattered throughout the republic. State authorities have classified the rural population into three categories: *lao lum* or lowlanders—mainly ethnic Lao who tend to occupy the lowland plains; *lao theung* or midlanders—who make up about 22 percent of the population and occupy the uplands; and *lao soong* or highlanders—dwellers of the highlands of over 1,000 meters.

Laos is also endowed with an abundance of water and productive inland fisheries, upon which the majority of local people depend for their daily sustenance. More than half of the rural population is engaged in swidden cultivation. Normally, farmers clear and cultivate small plots of hill farms for one year and then leave them fallow for the next seven to ten years. When the forest has fully regenerated, farmers will once again return to clear the plot for planting, often leaving large trees intact. Under this system of swidden agriculture, farming households may have as many as ten to fifteen plots of land in various stages of regrowth. Swidden farmers in Laos cultivate a prodigious diversity of crops and maintain one of the world's greatest shares of cultivated plants. Tropical Southeast Asia supports an unrivaled array of crop species and plant subtypes known as landraces, local varieties, or cultivars. In addition to swidden cultivation, Lao farmers depend on the forests and on fishing for most of their food supply throughout the year.

No longer the remote buffer state it was during the Cold War confrontation between the Soviet Union and America in Indochina, Laos is now a "crossroads state" (Evans 1995, xx) between the major powers of the Mekong Basin, all of whom are committed to supporting political stability in Laos for the expansion of market-based capitalist development in the subregion. Over the past two decades, Laos has increasingly attempted to transform itself from a self-sufficient socialist economy to a market-based economy. The consequence of this shift in economic policy is an increasing penetration of market forces into many sectors of the economy and the opening up of opportunities for resource exploitation.

In fact, the prospects for Laos to maintain even a semblance of control over the direction of its economic development look slim. Advisors from the World Bank, ADB, UNDP, and other donor organizations insist that Laos has no other option but to develop its hydropower resources and sell electricity to neighboring countries. These advisors, coupled with hydropower industry consultants, have promised huge influxes of foreign revenue that will help fuel economic development for the country, which is very poor in terms of GDP per capita (IRN 1999, 2). While achieving some short-term economic gains, however, many hydropower projects have resulted in widespread negative environmental and social impacts.

In recent years, a number of researchers and scholars (Hirsch and Choeng 1996, Phetsavanh 2004, Guttal and Shoemaker 2004, among others) have cautioned that Laos will soon be confronted with increasing development dilemmas stemming from resource-based economic growth. Environmental impacts from poorly conceived megaprojects are turning into livelihood threats, especially for the rural population. During a fact-finding trip to villages affected by the Nam Leuk Dam, Laotian researcher Phetsavanh Sayboualavan (2004) found that villagers in the area are suffering from problems related to food security, health, and education. Some villagers have been relocated and their agricultural land has been lost, resulting in negative social and livelihood impacts. Phetsavanh also found that water for drinking, agriculture, and transportation is now in short supply, especially in the dry season, due to dramatic changes in hydrology and water quality. More importantly, aquatic life, including fish, has been substantially reduced, making fishing and other river-based livelihood activities very difficult for riparian communities in the affected area. Unlike communities in the lower parts of the Nam Leuk basin which face water shortages, people living near the Nam Xan River who are the recipients of water from the Nam Leuk Dam have to deal with too much water. The poor quality of water from the reservoir causes massive fish die-offs as well as various health problems for humans and domestic animals.

A number of hydropower projects in Laos, for example the Nam Leuk Dam (Phetsavanh 2004a) and the Xe Pian–Xe Nam Noy Hydro-electric Project (Phetsavanh 2004b, Roberts and Baird 1995) have been constructed without the consent of stakeholder communities. Despite assurances from the government, there are serious on-going problems with mitigation of the social and environmental impacts of many hydropower projects. One paper, "Manufacturing Consent," (Guttal and Shoemaker 2004) has strongly criticized the Nam Theun 2 hydropower project for its devastation of prime forest and agricultural lands, the involuntary relocation of thousands of local villagers, and the possible impacts on ecosystems of two large river basins and the livelihoods of tens of thousands of farmers and fisherfolk who depend on these resources for their survival. The government of Laos, according to these authors, calculates the benefits of megaprojects in terms of generating electricity for sale to neighboring countries, while completely neglecting lessons learned from past failures of dams, especially in terms of the severe social, environmental, and economic impacts on local people.

In a comprehensive review of seven hydropower projects in Laos in 1999, International Rivers Network (IRN 1999) characterized hydropower development in Laos as a "flawed process" in urgent need of reform. All seven of the hydropower projects reviewed shared similar fundamental problems, including resettlement under very poor conditions, uncontrolled logging, inadequate compensation for affected villagers, and problems with regulation and the conducting of environmental impact assessments. IRN also voiced concern that the dependence of Lao people on their rivers for all aspects of life— including drinking water, fish, and aquatic animals for protein, irrigation, and fertilization of crops, transportation, and recreation— renders them highly vulnerable to the very substantial changes in the river systems brought about by hydropower megaprojects, and that these costs may outweigh any economic benefits.

Uncontrolled logging in dam construction areas is closely related to hydropower projects. In Laos, where the preservation of forests is already under threat, the construction of dams provides additional impetus for further degradation. As the forestry sector is a major source of revenue and export income, decisions ranging from forest policy down to logging concession approvals are centralized at the highest level of authority. Despite the fact that logging concessions have been one of the major causes of forest degradation, the government points the finger at highland shifting cultivators as the main culprits. To curb shifting cultivation, the land–forest allocation program was implemented in the 1990s to prevent watershed, forestry, and ecological degradation, particularly in mountainous areas (Kham Lee 2003, 118). In a participatory assessment of poverty conducted by the ADB at the beginning of the new millenium, however, the program was identified by rural villagers as a major cause of poverty. The shortened fallow periods introduced by the program have resulted in soil degradation and a decrease in rice yields (Mingsarn 2003, 100).

The collapse of socialism and the rapid rise of capitalist expansionism have resulted in the absence of a coherent agrarian policy in the wake of a decline in rural self-reliance. There is a widespread perception that the standard of living in rural Laos is inadequate and that poverty is widespread. The Lao government has given up on any strategy to extract agricultural surplus from rural areas to finance development. The government now looks to outside markets, hoping to increase export earnings and revenues from sales of energy and timber and from tourism. The Lao government has pinned its national economic future on hydroelectricity export earnings, joining with international consortia made up of private companies and state-owned utilities to develop large-scale hydroelectricity projects along practically every major river in the country. While these projects may or may not result in "development" in the real sense of improved livelihoods, greater productivity, infrastructure and services, there is no doubt they will bring with them the administrative and coercive machinery of the state. More importantly, the circular logic here is that to the extent livelihoods are not improved, projects fail

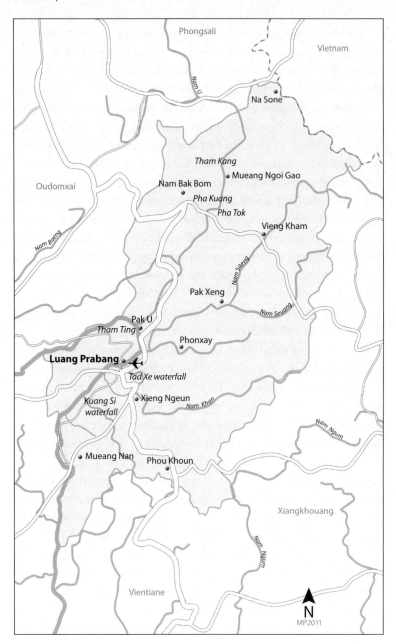

Map of Luang Prabang Province

to produce, services are poor, and local people recalcitrant, this only proves that a stronger state presence and more development projects are required. Riparian communities are particularly threatened by these hydropower development projects because most do not have state-sanctioned rights to the resources upon which they ultimately depend.

Marginal Communities in Luang Prabang

Located at the convergence of the Mekong, Nam Khan, Nam Ou, and Nam Seung in northern Laos, Luang Prabang has become a major tourist destination since 1995, when UNESCO put the former capital city on the World Heritage List. Despite the booming tourism industry, fish and other aquatic resources from the Mekong and its tributaries remain of overriding importance for surrounding rural communities, particularly given the lack of alternative sources of protein for much of the population.

Fisheries are clearly one of the most important livelihood resources for local communities in Luang Prabang, and their relative importance may be increasing, particularly in areas where rice production does not provide families with a sufficient supply of food for the entire year. In these areas, wild capture fisheries in the Mekong and its tributaries are the main livelihood. Fisheries are also a significant component of the local economy. Traders from the city travel to riverside villages to buy fish on a regular basis, with some riparian villages selling hundreds of kilograms or more per day.

In addition to fish, many other aquatic resources are gathered from rivers and wetlands by villagers, although the amounts and types of resources harvested differ from village to village. They include shrimp, snails, weeds, frogs, crabs, and aquatic insects and are collected for daily consumption by local villagers. A great deal of income is also gained from their sale. The cultivation of riverbank vegetable gardens is a further important livelihood activity for villagers in Luang Prabang. Produce from riverbank gardens contributes to family food supplies, while the surplus is sold at local markets.

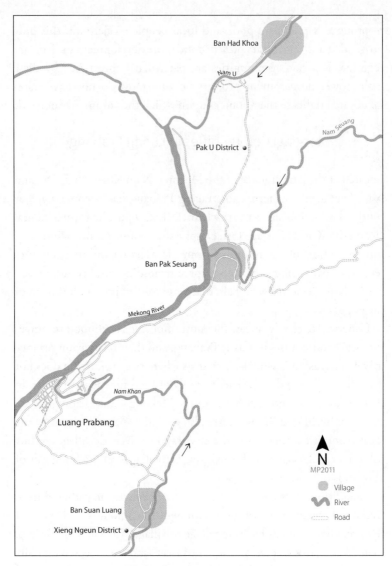

Map of research sites in Luang Prabang Province

Because the Mekong River and its tributaries are the principle source of livelihood and economic security for local communities, hydropower projects have serious implications for fisheries and agriculture. In recent years, villagers have reported declines in fish catches ranging from 30 to 60 percent. They also complain about soil erosion which results in the loss of riverbank vegetable gardens.

The remainder of this chapter describes the river-based livelihoods of riparian communities in Luang Prabang and the impacts of changes in hydrology on the livelihoods of local people. Data are derived from field research in three villages in Luang Prabang: Ban Suan Luang, on the banks of Nam Khan River; Ban Pak Seung, located at the mouth of Nam Seung River; Ban Hat Kho, a small riparian community located on the banks of Nam Ou River.

Luang Prabang Province has a tropical monsoon climate with considerable temporal variation in rainfall. Of the approximate 1,400 millimeters of average annual rainfall, more than 90 percent falls during the hot and humid months of May to October. Luang Prabang is predominantly mountainous, consisting mainly of hills and steep to very steep slopes. Flat and gentle slopes represent less than one percent of the total land area.

Traditional house in Ban Suan Luang

Elevation varies from 290 to 2,257 meters above sea level. Luang Prabang farmers live in small villages of around one to two hundred households. Lowland villages are composed of several hamlets and often lie alongside major rivers.

Traditional houses are constructed of wood and bamboo, and raised on stilts. Lao farmers

A riparian village in Luang Prabang on a newly paved road

usually surround their houses with small gardens and fruit orchards for subsistence consumption. Their most important resources are the rain-fed paddy land and hill farms on which they grow the annual staple crop of glutinous rice. In addition to agriculture, most households engage in harvesting forest products, hunting, animal husbandry, and fishing.

Most villages have well-established access and use rights to the forest and agricultural land within areas under their traditional control. A villager who clears a specific plot of land enjoys traditional usufruct rights over it. Rights are transmitted by way of inheritance or sale. Proprietal rights may only be maintained through continued cultivation. Prolonged lack of use or abandonment of a plot of land exempts the owner from all rights. The strength of kinship bonds in the village modifies the character of one's land rights. In fact, resource use is traditionally regulated through kinship systems or a council of village elders. A forest in which swidden plots are cultivated is generally regarded as belonging to the community, while the harvest derived from a specific plot is considered a private or household-based product. Other resource use, such as fishing in rivers, harvesting forest products, grazing livestock on grasslands, growing vegetables in riverbank gardens, and seasonal maintenance of irrigation channels, is regulated by resource user groups within and between villages. Riparian communities, for instance, have legends and rules governing the timing, spacing, and types of fish traps allowed in their waters.

All studies available on the Lao peasantry prior to the 1975 revolution report that there was little social differentiation in village life. Peasant villages have been described as having "a social structure which is little differentiated because one only has to clear land in order to meet a growth in household needs" (Evans 1995, 36–37). In general, the majority of Lao farmers continued to live and work in a natural economy until the mid-1960s. The main reason for the persistence of an un-differentiated natural economy was poor internal economic integration due to the rugged terrain and poor quality of transportation routes. Consequently, there was no truly national economy in Laos. Lao peasants produced very little economic surplus and engaged in little commercial activity.

The Indochina war contributed to the destruction of natural resources as well as a breakdown in traditional property regimes. After the war, the national government first territorialized state control over natural resources when it came to power in 1975, declaring that all land and resources belonged to the people and would be held in public trust. In reality, however, extraction of commercial timber under several military-run forestry enterprises accelerated rapidly, leading to rapid deterioration of forest land. The Lao government shared the perception held elsewhere in the Mekong Basin that shifting cultivation is environmentally destructive and economically unproductive and thus another major cause of forest destruction. The government estimated that 340,000 families of highlanders were practicing shifting cultivation throughout the country and announced its intention to reduce that number by 60 per cent by the year 2000. By restricting swidden practices, the government was hoping to accelerate the conversion of land for subsistence rice production to market-oriented forestry.

In the early 1990s, the Lao government embarked upon an ambitious 'Mob Din Mob Paa' land-forest allocation program. This program contained a number of new and challenging concepts. First of all, organizing teams were sent to initiate discussions with local villages, different land types are identified, and village maps indicating forest and farm lands drawn. Based upon these maps, forest and farm land was allocated to individual households. To stimulate investment in land development as well as the stability of livelihood, the land-forest allocation program stipulated new legal rights such as the right of possession, right to use, usufruct rights, right to transfer, right of inheritance, and right to receive compensation by the state. The program was launched with the goal of reducing and gradually eradicating shifting cultivation, and strengthening food security and agricultural production by taking land-forest allocation as a point of departure for focusing on the preservation of forest and the environment. The program, also aims at transforming a subsistence-based economy into a commercial economy by strengthening local management practices in protecting, managing, and enriching forest and farm lands for cash crop production. Land not suitable for agricultural production is also allocated to individual families for tree planting.

The decree that has most adversely affected shifting cultivators and their traditional access to forests for the purpose of swidden cultivation is the land law of 1992. This law stipulates that land left fallow for longer than three years can be claimed by the state for reforestation. In addition, the 1996 law entrenches state allocation of land rights to families only for "fixed agriculture." Since then, government agencies have begun to limit the number of swidden plots to four per family, allowing for three year fallows, rather than the customary seven to ten year fallow period. The effect of restricting the numbers of swidden plots has been declining crop yields, soil erosion, weed infestation, and rice shortages.

The combination of the land-forest allocation policy promoting private property rights for resource management, the government policy of moving highland communities to the lowlands, policies on eliminating shifting cultivation, and claims on forests for conservation and commercial forestry, have resulted in increased land pressure in both highland and lowland communities in Luang Prabang. Because of increasing land pressure, peasants are forced to intensify land use by reducing the fallow period. As a result, crop yields have declined, and erosion depletion of soil nutrients and organic matter have resulted in less fertile soil being available for agriculture. Ironically, these policies which aim to protect the environment and conserve land resources, have in fact "artificially decreased agricultural land availability and made farming practices unsustainable."

Ban Suan Luang

Traditionally, population growth in rural areas had been accommodated through the clearing of new land and the formation of new villages. Over the past decade, these mechanisms have failed to function, and population pressure has begun to build up on the Luang Prabang

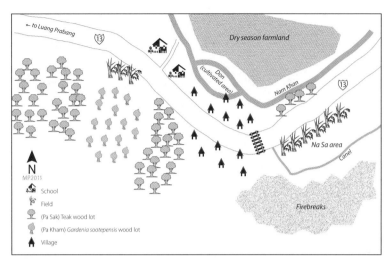

Map of Ban Suan Luang

plain. In many riparian villages, the population has increased rapidly. Ban Suan Luang, on the Nam Khan River, is a fine case in point.

Ban Suan Luang—Suan Luang village—was originally called Ban Na Sa. It's settlement began many decades ago, and the population increased from 15 households of lowlanders in 1946 to 85 households in 1966. Suan Luang was formally recognized in 2000 by the authorities of Muang Chiang Ngen, a district in the province of Luang Prabang, when it was merged with two relocated villages, Ban Na Sa and Ban Si Mongkol. Since then, the village has undergone a series of immigration phases and today is home to some 265 households with 1,647 inhabitants. While a large proportion of the people living in the riparian villages of Luang Prabang are ethnic Lao, the government policy of moving highland and midland communities down to the lowlands has resulted in the resettlement of displaced peoples into multi-ethnic villages. In Suan Luang, highlanders and midlanders have been forced down into the valleys and integrated into hamlets with ethnic Lao.

Ban Suan Luang is comprised of residents from the government's three main ethnic categories in comparatively equal numbers. There are 102 households of *lao lum* (ethnic Lao), 74 households of *lao theung*

Cash crops are cultivated in paddy fields after the rice harvest.

(mostly Khmu) and 89 households of *lao soong* (mostly Hmong and Mien). Each of these groups has their own linguistic and cultural characteristics, but in recent years, the relocated *lao theung* and *lao soong* have begun to assimilate with the *lao lum*. Many have taken up Buddhism and no longer practice animism. Their children now mainly speak Lao.

Ban Suan Luang residents engage in a variety of agricultural activities. Seventeen *lao lum* households, most of which are descendants of the first settlers who founded the village, cultivate wet rice. In addition, twenty-two households are involved in upland rice production. Upland plots are now cultivated for one or two successive years before allowing a three-year fallow period. Cropping usually begins in February when vegetation on fallow plots is cleared. In March, the fields are burned.

A wide variety of crops are planted in the upland swidden fields, but rice is the primary crop. Each field contains a number of different varieties of rice that are classified as heavy, medium, and late ripening; by color and shape of the grain (short, long, golden, red, or yellow); and by source of germplasm (for instance, rice varieties obtained from other places or other ethnic groups). In Suan Luang, the most commonly planted varieties are glutinous, heavy, and slow maturing types with a fairly short, rounded grain. Each household normally plants eight to ten different varieties of swidden rice, and keeps their own seeds separate from all other rice, preferring it to that of other households. Poorer families, who cannot afford to wait the extra month for heavy rice to mature, plant large amounts of light and early-ripening rice varieties.

The planting of different varieties of rice over a three to four week period is highly beneficial when it comes to harvest time because different ripening dates reduce the amount of labor needed to harvest. Different varieties of rice and ripening dates also reduce the risk of total production loss due to pests or unseasonal storms near harvest time. Several varieties of flowers, maize, beans, mustard, taro, sweet potatoes, yams and other tubers, as well as many varieties of melons, cucumbers, gourds, and squash are also grown in the swidden farms. Each variety of crop is planted according to its growth habits, and soil and water requirements.

In recent years, the average land holding in Ban Suan Luang has declined markedly. Whereas each household traditionally held ten to fifteen swidden plots, today those numbers have dropped to three to five plots per household. Increasing land pressure is forcing Suan Luang residents to shorten their cultivation-fallow cycle from eight to ten years to three years. Predictably, this change has resulted in the destabilization of subsistence security and may lead to further changes in swidden practices as villagers face the expected problems arising from short fallow periods.

Despite the relative familiarity of wet rice cultivation and upland cropping in the region, it is cash crop production in riverbank vegetable gardens rather, which constitutes the single most important livelihood activity—for ninety-three Ban Suan Luang households, most of which have neither paddy land nor upland farms. For these villagers, produce from riverbank vegetable gardens is a major contribution both to family food supplies and cash income. The riverbank vegetable garden is a traditional agro-ecosystem of great importance for poorer and landless villagers in Ban Suan Luang.

Riverbank gardens on the Nam Khan

In recent years, increasing land pressure has led Suan Luang residents to diversify their occupations. Following the rice harvest, a farmer may perform wage-labor for several months. Increasing numbers of Suan Luang residents now work outside the village as civil servants, traders, and construction workers. Families typically have members working as bus drivers, hawkers, and maids in Luang Prabang. The raising of livestock, especially cattle, goats, pigs, and poultry, has also increased, as has plantation production and several non-agricultural activities such as craftwork and weaving. Vegetable cropping has increased sharply to meet the needs of the expanding tourist industry.

Table 4.1: Distribution of Households and Farmland

Village	No. of Households	GDP	Paddy Farming Only	Hill Farming Only	Paddy Farming and Hill Farming
Hat Kho	124	1,920,000 kip/person	10 households/ 9.30 hectares	65 households/ 60 hectares	49 households/ paddy 14.59 hectares, hill farm 39.2 hectares
Pak Seung	103	2,400,000 kip/person	25 households/ 22 hectares	20 households/ 20 hectares	–
Suan Luang	265	1,800,000 kip/person	17 households/ 17.65 hectares	22 households/ 34.70 hectares	–

Table 4.2: Primary Occupations and Secondary Sources of Income

Village	Primary Occupation							Secondary Sources of Income	
	Rice Production	Riverbank Cash Crop Production	Traders	Animal Husbandry	Bus Drivers	State Officials	Construction Workers	Weaving	Fishing
Hat Kho	124	-	-	30	-	5	5	45	69
Pak Seung	45	30	10	3	5	5	5	-	86
Suan Luang	39	93	21	27	11	35	9	20	34

Ban Pak Seung

Ban Pak Seung, or Pak Seung village, is located at the convergence of the Nam Seung and the Mekong, eighteen kilometers from Luang Prabang. Settlement of Ban Pak Seung began 200 years ago when a few families of *lao lum* founded the village. In 1968, a number of families from Muang Hum, Muang Bang, and Vientiane also fled the war and settled in Pak Seung. Today, Pak Seung is home to some 103 households with 567 inhabitants. Residents are predominantly *lao lum*, with 4 households of *lao theung* and 2 households of *lao soong*.

Ban Pak Seung residents are predominantly subsistence farmers and fishermen. Twenty-five households cultivate wet rice and twenty households are involved in upland rice production. Fish and other aquatic resources from the Mekong and Nam Seung are of overriding importance, increasingly so as rice production no longer provides most families with a sufficient supply of food for the entire year. Eighty-six Pak Seung households are involved in the fish trade. Wild capture fisheries in the Mekong and Nam Seung are their main means of livelihood and a significant component of the village economy. Local fish traders travel from Pak Seung to deliver fish to customers in Luang Prabang on a

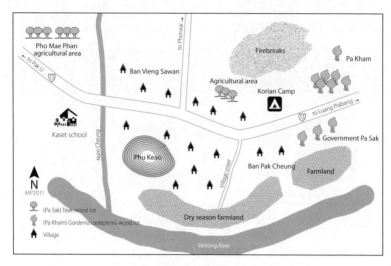

Map of Ban Pak Seung

regular basis. On average, each household sells one to two kilograms of fish per day.

In addition to fish, villagers gather many other aquatic resources from the rivers and wetlands. These aquatic resources include shrimp, snails, aquatic plants, frogs, crabs, and edible insects. The cultivation of riverbank vegetable gardens along the Mekong and Nam Seung is an important livelihood activity for thirty Pak Seung households. Produce from the riverbank gardens contributes to their family food supplies, while the surplus is sold at the local market. Cash crop production in riverbank vegetable gardens and hill farms, especially of oranges, bananas, corn, and

Riverbank gardens on the Nam Seung

other marketable produce, has now replaced rice production, and constitutes an important livelihood activity for thirty Ban Pak Seung households. As in Ban Suan Luang, but to a lesser degree, increasing land pressure has led Ban Pak Seung residents to diversify their livelihood strategies.

Ban Hat Kho

Ban Hat Kho, is located at the mouth of Nam Ou, 35 kilometers from Luang Prabang. Settlement of Hat Kho began 600 years ago when a few Tai Lue families from Sipsong Panna founded the village. Since 1975, the village has undergone a series of immigration phases with the relocation of villagers into Ban Hat Kho from Hat Pang, Lat Ta Rae, and Hat Ya. Today, Hat Kho is home to some 124 households with 655 inhabitants. Residents fall into two of the government's ethnic categories. There are 118 households of *lao lum*, and 6 households of *lao soong*.

Compared to Ban Suan Luang and Ban Pak Seung, Ban Hat Kho is located further from the city, and is less dependent on the cash economy. Hat Kho residents are predominantly subsistence farmers and fishermen. Fewer families have members working in Luang Prabang. Ten households cultivate wet rice and sixty-five households are involved in upland rice production. In addition, forty-nine households have both paddy land and hill farms. Fish and other aquatic resources from the

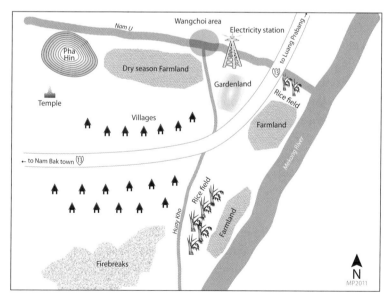

Map of Ban Hat Kho, Pak U, Luang Prabang

A local fisherman casts a net to fish in the Nam Seung

Fishing with nets in the Nam Ou

Mekong and Nam Ou are of over-riding importance to Ban Hat Kho residents. Thirty-eight households are involved in the fish trade. Wild capture fisheries on the Mekong and Nam Ou are their main means of livelihood. Prawn fishing is also of considerable economic significance to Hat Kho residents.

According to local villagers, the fishing season begins around June, when water levels and flow volumes in the mainstream rivers begin to increase. It is around this time that a large number of fish species begin migrating up the Nam Seung, Nam Khan, and Nam Ou from the Mekong, and other fish species move out from their dry season habitats in deep pools.

At this time of year, each household is able to catch large amounts of fish, providing a sizable income of 300,000 to 400,000 kip. The main species caught at both the beginning and the end of the rainy season are *pa kheung, pa khe, pa sakang, pa pak, pa na*, and *pa nang*. *Pa doke keo, pa ka, pla khe, pa phia, pa sakang,* and many other fish species migrate up the Nam Ou, Nam Seung, and Nam Khan in Laos from the Mekong River. Some of these fish, such as *pa doke keo*, are not seen during any other season.

The beginning of the rainy season is also the time that local fishermen on the Nam Seung and Nam Ou make a substantial income from freshwater prawns. When mainstream rivers become highly turbid due to heavy rainfall, the prawns move up out of the river into *bo*—cool, crystal clear streams that issue from caves at the base of riverside hills. These short migrations take place at night, and local fishermen intercept the prawns by placing *sai* traps along the sides and middle of the *bos*. Traps are set in the late afternoon and the prawns are retrieved at dawn. Local fishermen claim that prawns only enter *bo*, and do not move up into other streams that carry surface run-off from rainfall. As soon as the turbidity decreases in the mainstream of the river, the prawns move back out of the *bo*, signaling the end of the prawn season. Individual fishermen can catch between two to ten kilograms of prawns per night over an approximate 120 day fishing season. In Luang Prabang, prawns sell for around 45,000 kip per kilogram, and a local fisherman can sell his catch to a village middleman for 35,000 to 40,000 kip per kilogram.

In riparian communities, women play a vital role in subsistence and economic activities. As the rainy season ends in late September, women participate in an important fishery activity based on migrating *pa soi*— small species of fish with scales approximately five to twenty centimeters in length. *Pa soi* are caught along the large tributaries using lift nets. This fishery lasts for about one to two weeks, but is crucial for the food security of every household. *Pa soi* are an integral ingredient in the making of *pa dak*, or fermented fish paste, which is consumed all year round. The *pa soi* season begins when the water starts to recede and migratory fish move out of rice fields, streams, swamps, and lakes to return to deep pools in the main rivers. Villagers set traps at the edges of paddy fields and on streams leading to the large tributaries. Large quantities of fish are caught, and villagers use most of these smaller fish to make *pa dak*. In the dry season, women collect *kai*—a high-protein freshwater algae found in submerged rapids, on pebbles, and along rocky beaches—for family consumption and for sale.

Woman collecting *kai* in the river

Changing Livelihood Activities

Vast numbers of riparian communities in Luang Prabang make their living through a mixture of wet rice and swidden agriculture, forest extraction, and fisheries. In recent years, communities have witnessed road construction, crop intensification, capital investment, deforestation, and relocations of people on a scale unparalleled in contemporary times. With these developments have come fundamental changes in the rural economy, polity, and morality as farmers respond to new pressures and take advantage of new opportunities.

Over the past decade, river-based livelihood activities of riparian communities in Luang Prabang have been affected by three closely-related factors: (1) increasing land pressure resulting from government policies; (2) increasing demands on natural resources resulting from tourism and an increasing penetration of market forces into many sectors of the economy; and (3) dramatic changes in hydrology and water quality resulting in part from upstream hydropower projects.

Increasing land pressure in riparian communities results in stress on local farming systems. Farmers develop adaptive strategies by changing and diversifying their land use and by modifying their cultivation practices. In Ban Hat Kho, where residents are predominantly subsistence peasants and fishermen, most villagers still identify rice-based agriculture —both lowland paddy cultivation and upland swidden cultivation—as their most important livelihood activity. In Ban Suan Luang, however, we have witnessed a marked change in farming systems. The rapid transformation resulting in part from intense land pressure is accompanied by a marked diversification of household livelihood strategies. Situated near a newly paved road with convenient access to the city, many Ban Suan Luang villagers have invested in vegetable cropping in Nam Khan riverbank gardens, and on paddy land and hill farms. Production of cash crops, especially cabbage, cauliflower, tomatoes, lettuce, mustard, chilies, and green peas, has become extremely important. All this produce is sold directly at the Luang Prabang market. Virtually all village households are now engaged in the raising of livestock—poultry, pigs, buffaloes, and cattle—for sale. More generally, village households have shifted from relatively specialized production to diversification. At the same time they have diversified their production, many households have also reduced their rice production and expanded cultivated areas for cash crops.

Increased demand from the growing tourism industry has led to a comparative advantage in cash crops such as cabbage, cauliflower, tomato, lettuce, green peas, and most importantly, a variety of tropical fruits such as bananas, oranges, and pomelos. In villages close to Luang Prabang, hill farms are being converted into home gardens and orchards that are the primary suppliers of the urban fresh food market. What follows in many farming villages in Luang Prabang is the emergence of increasing social differentiation. Rich farmers in Ban Pak Seung, for instance, are quick to respond to the opening of market opportunities by planting upland fields, many of them already eroded, with fruit trees in combination with traditional annual crops. Capital-poor peasants lacking the funds necessary for seedlings and chemical fertilizers, in contrast, face declining productivity, and are forced either to look for other opportunities such as off-farm employment and migration to urban centers, or to rely more heavily on subsistence activities such as fishing and gathering forest products.

The transition towards a market economy has increased farmers' needs for cash income, thereby promoting the production of cash crops. Increasing demands from the tourism industry has led to a tremendous increase in the number of villagers catching fish for the market, and larger nets are more prevalent today. The transition towards cash-oriented production is simultaneously encouraged through official policy, as implemented by agricultural and forestry officials. The expansion of new markets in the city of Luang Prabang has also led to new opportunities for non-agricultural employment. Thus the expansion of economic activities in Luang Prabang has played a vital role in changing livelihood activities for rural residents of riparian communities.

The growth of labor-intensive cash crops and the increase in off-farm employment are adaptations consistent not only with the expansion of new market opportunities, but also with rising population densities, increasing land pressure, and the growing need for economic alternatives to cope with simultaneous declines in agricultural productivity. On the surface, it appears that population growth may be the primary agent for much of these livelihood activity changes, but a closer analysis suggests that these demographic changes have resulted from top-down development policies and resettlement schemes rather than natural population growth.

Forests have been essential to rural communities in Laos for centuries. These forests include the seasonally flooded riverine forests along the Mekong, Nam Khan, Nam Ou, and Nam Seung, as well as dry-land forests. Flooded riverine forests are extremely important for maintaining a vibrant aquatic ecosystem. They are important sources of food and organic nutrients eaten by fish and other aquatic animals. Flooded forests are an essential part of food webs, playing a vital role in reducing riverbank erosion and providing shade that keeps the water relatively cool for fish. Apart from providing habitat and spawning grounds for a wide variety of fish, these forests are also home to many species of mammals, birds, amphibians, insects, shrimp, and reptiles.

Dry-land forests include evergreen, mixed deciduous, and dry dipterocarp forests. Villagers rely on a large number of non-timber forest products for subsistence needs from these. Dry-land community forests provide local people with vital resources: food, fuel wood, and construction materials. The gathering of edible products from forests is usually the responsibility of women and children. In the evenings,

women and their daughters often spend time together in the nearby forests gathering *pak* for cooking meals. *Pak* normally refers to various species of tender growth from trees in the forests. Local people identify more than a hundred different *pak* available in different seasons. At the beginning

Flooded forest on the banks of the Nam Ou

of the rainy season, villagers collect and sell *no mai* (bamboo shoots), *yod vai* (young rattan shoots) and a wide variety of *hed* (mushrooms) for substantial income. Other important dry forest products include small game, birds, honey, wild fruit, spices, medicinal herbs, resins, and latexes, as well as construction materials such as bamboo, wood for poles, rattan, and various fibers. Hunting activities are usually the responsibility of men.

In recent years, increasing land pressure in Luang Prabang has led to overexploitation of forest resources by landless peasants. Consequently, many community forests have been destroyed or degraded by timber harvesting, illegal logging, and the expansion of fruit orchards. In Luang Prabang, the added impetus from tourism and the increasing penetration of market forces into rural areas has resulted in an increased demand for wild captured fish and shrimp from the Mekong and its tributaries, but the transition to cash-oriented production has forced capital-poor peasants who lack economic alternatives to rely more heavily on subsistence production such as fishing and gathering forest products for cash income. While over the past decade, the demand for fish in Laos has increased in line with economic growth of 6 to 10 percent per annum, there appears to be a general decline in fish stocks. In all three villages studied, local fishermen report that fish stocks appear to be declining, partially as a result of over-fishing. Poorer community members are pressured to depend more on rivers, while rich villagers buy fish from local fishermen and sell them to restaurants and markets in Luang Prabang.

Can, a fifty-one-year-old fisherman in Ban Pak Seung, commented: "Many villagers these days devote much of their time and energy to fishing all year round. In the dry season, a number of villagers even fish during the night, using *sadoung* (lift nets), *bet* (lines), and a wide variety of fish traps. They return to the village each morning to sell their catch to local fish traders. At times, fishing trips last for a number of days and involve camping on the banks of the river during the night. More and more villagers are involved in the fish trade since they lack other alternatives."

Poorer community members are also pressured to find new livelihood activities such as through the expansion of hill farms by clearing forest land, and increased timber harvesting, and the hunting and wildlife trade. In many villages, natural forests have declined and the forestland that remains is under threat, due both to timber harvesting and the expansion of farms and grazing areas. In many places, for example in Suan Laung, where complex systems of forest management and user rights were traditionally enforced by moral codes, these systems are being challenged and conflicts are arising from both within and outside the community. In general, community-based forest management has been eroded by the government policies of land-forest allocation and the promotion of household-based commercial forestry. Traditional concepts of harmonious coexistence between people and the forest are being replaced by forest plantations, timber production, and income generation.

As the poorer members of riparian communities in Luang Prabang are pressured to increasingly exploit the forests and rivers for their survival, dramatic changes in hydrology and water quality resulting in part from upstream hydropower projects have wreaked havoc on the natural rhythm of water levels and fish migration. A local fisherman in Ban Pak Seung commented: "As of recent years, we can no longer be certain of the Mekong's water levels. At times, the water changes so rapidly and unpredictably that we can barely catch up. Every dry season, the Mekong recedes more and more, and the water level has dropped considerably. The unnatural flow of water could have an impact on a number of fish species, especially the migrators. As more and more people are depending on fisheries for their livelihoods, fish stocks are declining rapidly, due to both over-fishing and changes in the river system."

The unnatural flow of water has greatly affected many livelihood activities of local villagers. Over the past few years, Ban Pak Seung villagers have noticed a decrease in *kai*. Usually, *Kai* grows during the dry season in submerged rapids, on pebbles, and along rocky beaches. For three months in the dry season, villagers collect *kai* for household consumption and for sale. "We used to be able to earn quite a bit of money selling *kai* to traders," commented a housewife from Ban Suan Laung. "But in recent years, we have noticed that it's becoming more and more difficult to find it."

The practice of riverbank gardening, so important to the livelihood of the landless peasants in Luang Prabang, is also threatened by massive hydroelectric schemes. The construction of additional mainstream dams in Yunnan could spell disaster for the future viability and productivity of riverbank gardens, not only in Luang Prabang but along the entire length of the Mekong. These dams will radically alter the hydrology of the Mekong, causing greater dry season flows and diminished wet season flows. Greater dry season flows means that traditional riverbank cropping areas will be periodically inundated.

Changes in hydrology will also adversely affect deep pools in the Mekong and its tributaries. Deep pools have long been recognized by local peoples as a refuge for migrating fish species during the dry season. Certain migratory species use the deep pools as spawning grounds. Some local species may spend their entire life-cycle in these habitats, preying on migrating fish. The pools are also important dry season refuges for many endangered fish species, including the giant Mekong catfish *Pangasianodon gigas* (Mekong River Commission 2005, 3) Riparian communities understand the vital importance of deep pools as habitats and spawning grounds for many fish species, and recognize the role they play in maintaining the vitality of fish ecology. Some riparian communities have long-established fish conservation zones to protect deep pools in their localities. In Ban Hat Kho on the Nam Ou, for instance, villagers have a fish management program that has three fish conservation zones. Strict rules on timing and the types of fishing gear allowed are enforced by the entire community. All fishing activities are prohibited during the spawning season. In certain conservation zones, only one *mong* (gill net) per family is allowed, and a fee of 5,000 kip is imposed on transgressors.

Despite the efficacy of these local management systems, however, any alteration of the river's ecosystem and natural hydrologic regime resulting from hydropower projects or flood mitigation schemes threatens the preservation of deep pools. Changes in the flow of the river may cause the deep pools to fill with silt or sediment slumping from increased riverbank erosion. Degradation of deep pools may have even more serious consequences than the often cited blockage of migration routes caused by dams. Clearly, any development scheme that alters the hydrology of the river threatens deep pool habitats.

More than twenty memoranda of understanding have been signed for hydropower projects in Laos, with an additional seventeen hydropower schemes awaiting memoranda of understanding. At least five of these projects are in Luang Prabang. Large-scale dams in both Laos and Yunnan could cause irretrievable changes to the Mekong River and its tributaries. These changes include the loss of fish and aquatic animals essential to riparian communities, the degradation of deep pools and river ecology, impedance to migrating fish, and changes in hydrology and water quality. For many fishing communities in Laos, these changes now constitute everyday life experience. The dramatic changes in hydrology and water quality resulting from upstream hydropower projects, coupled with increasing deforestation, are making fishing and other livelihood activities increasingly difficult, especially for riparian communities. Poorer families are forced to expand their swidden farms to cope with the lack of alternative food sources. In many areas, the decline in fish and aquatic animals is leading to rapid exploitation of forest resources for local survival.

FIVE

The Giant Catfish and Riparian Communities in Northern Thailand

In the stretch of river between Thailand's Hat Khrai and Lao's Huai Xai villages, local fishermen on both side of the river have been catching the Mekong giant catfish (*Pangasianodon gigas*), one of the world's largest freshwater fish, for generations. This is because the half-kilometer shoal of Don Waeng divides the Mekong here, narrowing its channel. The riverbed in this area is flat, making it an ideal place for laying nets. It is one of a few places along the entire length of the Mekong where fishermen have historically caught giant catfish for a living (Piyaporn 2003, 13). The hunting of giant catfish, knowledge of fishing gear and nets, and the annual ceremony to worship the guardian spirits of the river are all parts of a way of life that has been passed down from generation to generation. For more than a century, fishermen have keenly observed the natural rhythms of the Mekong, steadily improving their *mong* or nets to enable them to catch the 300 kilogram catfish.

Lung Saw, one of the most respected elderly fishermen of Ban Hat Khrai, was born in this village 80 years ago, The village is situated on the shores of the Mekong in Chiang Khong District, Chiang Rai Province, northern Thailand. Like his father before him, Lung Saw and his fellow villagers spent ten months of each year tending the rice fields and orchards. From the middle of April to the end of May, however, the men left their fields to catch *pla buek*, the Giant Catfish, in the Mekong.

Today, sacrifices and celebrations still mark the beginning and end of each fishing season. In Ban Hat Khrai, fishermen perform ritual sacrifices for the spirits of their boats. Boat owners pick up handfuls of rice and count the number of grains. If the number is even, it means the spirit of the boat prefers the sacrifice of a pig. If the number of grains is odd, the spirit of the boat prefers the sacrifice of a chicken. When a

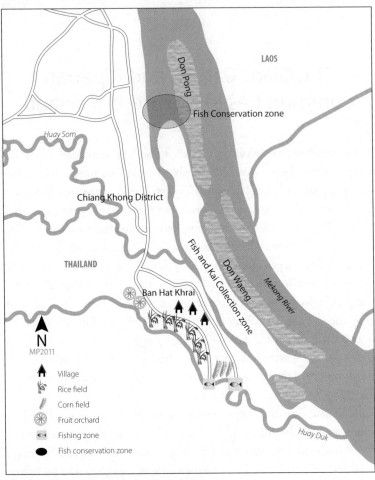

Map of Ban Hat Khrai on the shores of the Mekong

The ritual master prepares offering for the spirits.

catch is made, the spirits are offered a large meal of chicken or pork, glutinous rice, and homemade whiskey.

Before the giant catfish hunting season begins, local fisher folk hold the *liang luang* ritual, a merit-making ceremony to propitiate the spirits. On a mid-April morning, the smoke of incense and candles fills the air, mingling with the aroma of chicken and pork. The ritual master prepares the offering and chants a mantra accompanied by rhythmic northern Thai music to invoke the spirits. Villagers in this area believe that the giant catfish are protected by spirits, so the *liang luang* ritual is performed to ask permission to catch the fish with the blessings of the spirits. The history of the ritual harks back to 1877 when, according to local history, it was first performed.

In mid to late April, flocks of terns fly past Don Waeng, signaling the appearance of the giant catfish. Hat Khrai villagers often make their first catch by the first week of May. Tracking the consistent rise and fall of the water, local fishermen anticipate the river's depth and adjust their nets properly. The fishing season continues for a few weeks, as the water level rises, falls, then gradually rises again until June, when Don Waeng is again submerged, marking the end of the giant catfish season.

In the past, *pla buek* were caught solely for local consumption. Lung Saw still remembers when he was twelve years old, accompanying his father and other Hat Khrai fishermen on his first fishing trip. "In those days, we would sell one entire *pla buek* to Lao villagers at a price of 800 to 1,200 Baht. People on the Thai side didn't care much for them." However, in late 1970s, traders from Bangkok began coming to Chiang Khong to buy the giant catfish. High demand led to an increase in commercial fishing. Fishing for *pla buek* rapidly commercialized as Chiang Khong has been promoted as a tourist attraction and the fish publicized as a must-have culinary treat for tourists. From the early 1980s, the number of giant catfish captured by Hat Khrai villagers and their counterparts across the Mekong in Huai Xai steadily increased. In 1989 and 1990, the number of captured catfish reached its highest level, at 60 and 69 respectively.

In 2006, only one giant catfish was caught by Hat Khrai villagers.

The Manwan Dam was the first in a cascade of eight dams to be built upstream of Hat Khrai in southwest China's Yunnan Province. Shortly after the dam began generating electricity in 1994, Lung Saw began to notice a change in the Mekong's flow. In April of that year, the water dried up to about a meter in depth, and local fishermen caught only 18 giant catfish, compared to 48 in 1993. The following year, the level of the river in Chiang Khong District fell to 44 centimeters, its lowest recorded depth. "That was the first time in my life," says Lung Saw, "that I saw the Mekong's water dry up to the middle of the river." Dachaoshan Dam was built in 1997 and began operation in 2005. Xiaowan Dam, China's second largest after the Three Gorges Dam on the Yangtze River, and several other dams on the Lancang are now under construction. Since 1999, the fish catch has plummeted as the water levels have continued to rise and fell erratically, making it difficult to lay nets and catch fish.

According to statistics collected by the Southeast Asia Rivers Network (SEARIN), hydropower and other cross-border development projects have had a massive impact on the hydrology of the Mekong.

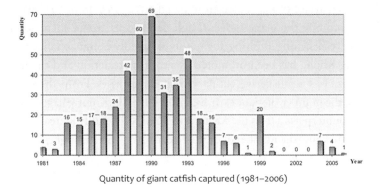

Quantity of giant catfish captured (1981–2006)

After the construction of Manwan Dam, the mean minimum discharge of the Mekong along the Thai-Lao border near Chiang Khong declined by 25 percent. According to Weerawut Pornrattanaphan, a hydrologist with the Water Resource Department of Thailand, upstream dams have caused a 25 percent decrease in the minimum discharge of the Mekong at Chiang Saen station. From 1962–1992, before the Manwan Dam was constructed, the mean minimum discharge was 752 CMS (cubic meters per second). From 1993–2003, however, the mean minimum discharge was only 569 CMS. These statistics illuminate a trend of long-term reduction in the minimum discharge. Over the long term, the volume of water in the Mekong will also decrease.

Together with the removal of rapids and shoals as part of the navigation improvement project, the construction and operation of a number of dams upstream causing unusually rapid water fluctuation, is leading to a massive decrease in food security for local people. Like Lung Saw, many fishermen from Ban Hat Khrai, Ban Pak Ing, Ban Muang Choom, and other villages along this eighty-four kilometer stretch of the Mekong in northern Thailand complain that they can no longer fish due to rapid water fluctuation, and that the number of fish, especially migratory species, has substantially declined. The rapid fluctuation and unnatural flow of water has also led to massive deterioration of the ecosystem, including riverbank erosion, the loss of riverbank gardens, and a declining stock of freshwater algae or *kai*, all of which are essential to local livelihoods.

Riverbank erosion along the Thai-Lao border in Chiang Saen and Chiang Khong

Today, Hat Khrai is home to 166 households. The majority of villagers are Tai Yuan lowlanders and the minority are made up of Lao, northeastern Thai, Yunnan Chinese, and Khmu. Ban Hat Khrai is located on the shores of the Mekong about one and a half kilometers from Chiang Khong District, and has benefited from the increasing number of tourists visiting this border town on the way to Huai Xai, Laos. A few well-to-do villagers have built guesthouses and restaurants on the banks of the Mekong to cater to both foreign and Thai tourists. In 1998, there were 597 people in 179 households in Hat Khrai. By 2005, the number of residents had decreased to 551 due to seasonal and permanent migration to urban areas.

Agricultural land in Ban Hat Khrai is fertile, with 1,253 *rai* (2.5 *rai* = 1 acre) of paddy fields, 895 *rai* of hill farms, and 89 *rai* of orchards. There is a large quantity of riverbank land where most villagers plant many vegetables and cash crops during the dry season. Although Hat Khrai has become part of Chiang Khong town and its tourist attraction, most villagers are still farmers, earning their main income from agricultural products including rice, corn, fruit, vegetables, and other cash crops. In addition to agriculture, about 10 percent of villagers have turned to trade as their main occupation, and another 10 percent have become wage laborers working outside the village.

Fisheries have long been a significant component of the local economy and one of the most important livelihood resources. Yet, fewer and fewer fishermen can be found in Hat Khrai these days. Declining fish stocks have put pressure on local fishermen to change their way of life from fishing to wage labor. Today, fishing is the main means of livelihood for only 15 percent of Hat Khrai villagers, and this percentage is declining every year. "Years ago, the giant catfish alone brought in at least several million Baht," says Lung Saw. "We've lost that income now. Fishing has become just a sideline job—we can't make a living from it." A survey of local villagers reveal that the number of fishermen has declined from 276 in 1987 to 32 in 1997 and 25 in 2006. In 2006, fishing brought in a total income of 275,000 baht for Hat Khrai fishermen.

In addition to the declining numbers of fish, Hat Khrai villagers are also losing income from the sale of *kai* and produce from their riverbank vegetables. In the middle of dry season, from late January to March, the Mekong recedes and the water becomes clearer, allowing optimum sunlight to reach the submerged rocks, rapids, and reefs. These are the ideal conditions for the rapid growth of *kai*. During this time, women collect this nutritious culinary treat for local consumption and for sale to tourists and outsiders. A Hat Khrai housewife lamented, "*Kai* is provided by nature and also helps to generate income for us. During the summer, we used to collect it three times a day and earn as much as four hundred to five hundred baht per day. There was a lot of *kai* then, but now it's gone." During the dry season, the women of Hat Khrai also utilize the beaches and sand dunes to grow vegetables for family consumption and sale. But the unnatural rise and fall in the level of the Mekong has robbed them of these important livelihood activities.

The people of Hat Khrai are not simply passive recipients of the development projects imposed upon them from the outside. The ecological deterioration of the Mekong, and the resulting decline of fish stocks, *kai* and riverbank gardens, has provided an impetus for the formation of a local conservation group named "Rak Chiang Khong," an alliance between local residents, fishermen, teachers, academics, and local and international NGOs. In a bid to simultaneously conserve endangered species, local hunting skills which are a part of ancestral traditions, and the fishermen's way of life, the conservation group has successfully called for a government-sponsored study of the giant catfish. Conservation zones on the Mekong have been clearly demarcated, and local fishermen have gradually been persuaded to stop fishing for giant catfish. In 2006, 69 fishermen from Ban Hat Khrai and other villages agreed to yield their fishing nets worth over 1.3 million baht, and the local giant catfish conservation group agreed to compensate them at 20,000 baht each. Funding comes mainly from wildlife conservation groups and the local government. Hat Khrai fishermen also requested that considerations be made for "demonstrating" giant catfish fishing on a very small scale for the purposes of cultural preservation, tourism, and research. The *liang luang* ritual to worship the guardian spirits also continues to be performed in mid-April of every year.

"Fishing for giant catfish is not just an occupation," says Lung Saw, "it is a way of life, a cultural heritage passed on for generations. We should conserve it."

Ban Pak Ing

Over the past decade, riparian communities in northern Thailand have undergone a dramatic transformation in livelihood strategies, food security and occupations. In response to the erratic fluctuation of water levels, riparian communities along the 84 kilometer stretch of the Mekong in Chiang Rai Province, northern Thailand have drawn upon their local knowledge of fish ecology and resource management, constantly adjusting it in order to preserve the life of the Mekong, its tributaries, and natural habitats. Numerous communities in Chiang Saen, Chiang Khong, and Wiang Kaen districts have established conservation zones and protected areas along the river.

The Ing River, a major tributary of the Mekong in northern Thailand

The Ing River is a major tributary of the Mekong in northern Thailand. It is about three hundred kilometers long and its flow varies seasonally. Flood waters from the Mekong inundate the Ing River Basin during the rainy season, spurring fish to enter the Ing for spawning. Intermittently flooded riverine forest and inland swamps and ponds on both sides of the Ing allow for ample spawning grounds for a wide variety of migratory fish. With the onset of the dry season, fish migrate back to the Mekong. In addition to agriculture, local people along the Ing River depend on fishing as one of their most important livelihood strategies. They rely upon seasonal fish migration and have learned to fish with great skill, particularly in the area's myriad inland swamps and ponds.

Ban Pak Ing lies at the intersection of the Mekong and Ing rivers. Local residents here are descendents of Lao settlers who migrated from Luang Prabang and other parts of northern Laos over a century ago. Pak Ing villagers traditionally grew rice and other cash crops such as corn, chilies, and beans. Tobacco was introduced to the area by the French

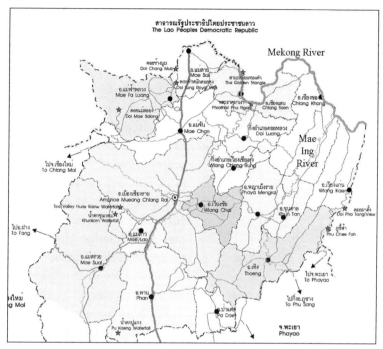

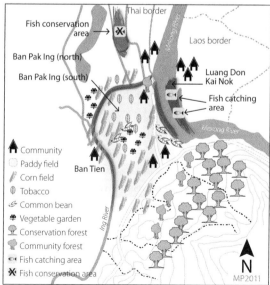

Map of the Ing River
in Chiang Rai Province

Map of Ban Pak Ing

Tobacco and other cash crops have become increasingly important to the livelihood of Ban Pak Ing residents since fishing has declined.

Fisherman from Ban Pak Ing at work on the Mekong River

colonial administration and is still a major cash crop for local residents. Over the past three decades, however, Pak Ing villagers have faced increasing land pressure as speculators have sought to buy land along the banks of the Mekong to build resorts, restaurants, and other projects. Consequently, many farmers now have to buy or rent land further away from the village for farming. Pak Ing literally means the mouth of the Ing, and local people depend on the richness of the river for their sub-sistence needs and income.

Pak Ing fishermen fish in both the Ing and Mekong rivers. They fish in the Ing during the rainy season when fish from the Mekong migrate to the Ing for spawning. When the fish return to the Mekong from November through March, fishermen turn their boats around to fish in the Mekong. Land scarcity and uncertain crop prices have made fishing the major income earning occupation for many Pak Ing residents. The abundance of wild capture fish from the Ing and Mekong rivers in this area has brought a substantial income for many fishermen. Fifteen years ago, fishermen could earn up to 100,000 baht a year from selling fish. Since 1993, however, the number of fish has dramatically declined.

In addition to declining fish stocks, riparian communities are increasingly facing the problem of riverbank erosion. At the turn of the millennium, riparian communities in the area cooperated to monitor soil erosion along the banks of the Mekong. In Ban Pak Ing alone, one acre of land disappeared in 2004. Nearby villages also suffered land loss from soil erosion. Unpredictable water fluctuation also makes it increasingly difficult for fish to migrate, leading to further declines in fish stocks.

In response to the erratic fluctuation of water levels, over two hundred fishermen in Ban Pak Ing decided to establish a two hundred meter no-fishing zone around the intersection of the Mekong and Ing rivers. "The amount of fish has been declining for years," commented Boonkong, the headman of Pak Ing village. "Young men and women have turned their backs on fishing and migrate to urban centers to work as wage laborers in search of a brighter future. But for many of the remaining residents, community bonds are still strong. We share the same goal, that is, to protect our environment and to revitalize the depleted food sources we used to be able to depend on."

The conservation zone has been a proud achievement for many villagers. Over the past few years, the fish population has gradually

The swamps and ponds of the Ing River Basin are important sources of protein for local residents. Certain swamps are under the tight control of local authorities and fishing is allowed only one day a year in order to conserve fish stocks.

made a comeback in the area. Local fishermen have adapted to the new regulations. They can now catch more fish than before outside the conservation area. "I don't mean to imply that we can fish full time like before," said the headman. "But the protected area increases our chances of being able to catch an adequate amount of fish for our children." The conservation area has become a fertile breeding ground for many varieties of fish.

During the rainy season, there are a couple of days when the water from both the Mekong and Ing rivers reach the same level. At this juncture, the confluence of the warmth of the Ing and the chill of the Mekong creates an ideal ground for fish to lay eggs. Because of the warmer temperature of the water, the fish from the Mekong spawn in the Ing River. Most of the fish caught in the Ing River during this time have migrated from the Mekong. The water from the Mekong not only floods the Ing River, but also inundates a great many inland swamps and ponds in Phaya Mengrai, Wiang Kaen, and Thoeng districts. Fish from the Mekong migrate and spawn in these swamps and form a significant component of the local economy. Fishing is one of the most important livelihood activities in these inland areas.

Fisheries along the Ing are dependant upon the annual flood cycle. During the rainy season, up to 40 percent of the total land area of the Ing River Basin is covered in water. At this time, few discrete

Fish from inland swamps are highly important to local economies.

bodies of water are discernable, and access to fisheries on the floodplains is traditionally open to all. However, once the flood water recedes to the extent that discrete residual bodies of water begin to appear, each village and subdistrict rigidly enforces their exclusive rights over access to specific fishing grounds. Thus local authorities—village committees and headmen—have total control over fishing gear used, and the timing and limitations on fishing. These local authorities can impose conservation and improvement measures as they wish. Mechanisms for community management of small village reservoirs include spawning habitat protection and timing control. Certain communities lease fishing rights to local fishermen only once a year. Community management is now seen by local governments as a viable way of making controls on fishing activities workable in practice, as well as distributing the benefits from fishing more equitably.

Fishing is a crucial source of livelihood for the 886,047 people living in the Ing River Basin, particularly low-income families in rural areas where job options are limited. Small-scale commercial and subsistence fishing often provides a last resort option when more lucrative labor opportunities cannot be found. The contribution of fisheries to the local food supply is also significant. From our survey, fish and fishery products constituted 20 percent of the total animal protein consumed by local people in Chiang Rai and Payao provinces in the Ing River Basin. The average consumption of fish and other aquatic animals is estimated at twenty-five kilograms per capita per year.

Although fisheries provide much needed protein and income, fishing has declined substantially over the years. Local villagers complain of declines in the total yield, and more and more species are becoming rare. This decline of fisheries takes place within a complex of factors. Local fishermen realize that overfishing is also an important factor (cf. Allen et al. 2005). From the local people's point of view, changes in hydrology and fish ecology resulting from large-scale transnational projects such as dam construction and reef blasting threaten both the biodiversity of the Mekong and its tributaries, and consequently the ecosystem of "goods and services" on which people rely. As long as the governments of the Mekong Basin are more concerned with infrastructural development and the promotion of transnational trade, the severity of this threat will be underappreciated. Local communities, on the contrary, may not be as nearsighted. Many riparian communities in northern Thailand are beginning to see the need to promote conservation measures. The practical effect of this new awareness is a widening of the group of stakeholders with legitimate interests in how natural resources are managed. The formation of networks and institutional structures that allow wider stakeholder participation in resource management is essential for the successful implementation of fishery management strategies.

Khun Huai Khrai: Upland Fisheries

For centuries, the northern region of Thailand has served as a refuge for ethnic minority groups including the Karen, Akha, Hmong, Htin, Khmu, Lahu, Lisu, and Mien, who have migrated to the region due to various political, economic, and other social pressures in their native lands. These migrations began in the mid-nineteenth century and continue today. There are now some 2,200 ethnic minority villages dispersed throughout the remote highland areas of northern Thailand.

Upland fishing in the Huai Khrai stream in the summer

Fisheries and aquaculture play an important role in the livelihoods of many of these upland peoples. The ways in which highlanders fish are linked to local conditions: in areas with streams, there is a lot of opportunity for fishing; where there is little access to streams, villagers rely on ponds to raise fish.

The Hmong of Khun Huai Khrai have long practiced upland fishing. Their ancestors migrated from Laos and established a village near a stream that was subsequently

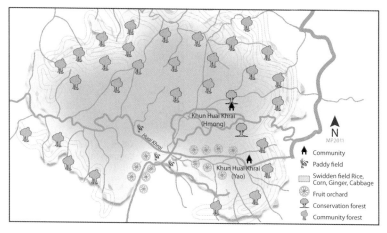

Map of Ban Khun Huai Khrai

named Huai Khrai. This stream is in the watershed of the Ngao, a major tributary of the Ing River; the village located about 130 kilometers south of the Mekong. While very limited data exists on upland fisheries in northern Thailand, we attempted to determine the level of dependence of the Hmong in Ban Khun Huai Khrai on fisheries, how they obtain fish and aquatic animals and the relative importance of fishing in Hmong livelihoods. We expected that the fish catch would be relatively low, since fishery resources in the highlands are not as good as those in the lowlands. Nevertheless, our survey of random households in the village shows that fishery resources are still significant in the livelihoods of the highlanders.

The highlands of Huai Khrai are home to several ethnic groups, predominantly the Hmong and Mien. Traditionally, members of these ethnic groups made a living mainly by growing hill rice for subsistence, and cash crops, including opium, for income. Production was based on a traditional system of shifting cultivation. The Hmong, like other ethnic minorities in the highlands of northern Thailand, traditionally favored high altitudes of over 1,000 meters where a mixed and semi-pastoral economy based on upland rice, maize, and poppy could best be practiced, together with animal husbandry, cultivation of fruit trees,

Ban Khun Huai Khrai, Chiang Rai
Province

Hmong swidden rice field surrounded by
community forests

fishing, hunting, and gathering (Tapp 1989: 16–17). In the early 1960s,
Communist insurgents were active along the Thai-Lao border. To
prevent the spread of Communism, the Thai military relocated the
Hmong and Mien villagers in this area to the lowlands. In the 1980s,
once ideological confrontations had subsided, the Hmong of Khun
Huai Khrai were allowed to return to their homes.

New cropping practices accompanied resettlement. Over the
following decades, a large number of development projects were initiated
to develop alternative forms of agriculture to replace opium. While large
amounts of money were invested, many independent observers (Cohen
1981, 1984; Dirksen 1997) have been critical of the benefits of these
projects. Cash cropping, nonetheless, began to spread through the
highlands, both as a direct and indirect result of these projects. By the
mid-1990s, opium growing had been radically reduced and today cash
crops are ubiquitous throughout the northern highlands. Forest cover
has fallen dramatically, as have wildlife populations (Woranoot and
Dearden 2002). Families with paddy land now practise wet rice
cultivation. Highland paddy fields are keenly sought after, though the
amount of flat land with sufficient water supplies for rice is limited. Dry
land cultivation therefore remains widespread, mostly on steep slopes.

With government restrictions on traditional mobility, highland
villages in this area have remained in the same location for more than
two decades. A growing upland population and a decline in the area
available for swidden farming has greatly reduced soil fertility. Food

Fruit orchards and rice fields situated behind the village

Fishing for larger fish with spears

security has thus become a major challenge. Many villagers have been forced to adopt more intensive methods of agricultural production. Hill rice, maize for animal fodder, and a large number of subsistence crops such as gourds, beans, vegetables, and root crops are grown in upland swidden fields. A lack of fallow rotation results in low yields and heavy weeding requirements. Highland farmers are reluctant to apply costly fertilizers and pesticides to subsistence crops, but use them on cash crops, especially cabbages, tomatoes, lettuce, and flowers. Cash crops are subject to erratic price fluctuations, however, and at times, simultaneous seasonal collapse of tomato and cabbage prices threatens the food security of poor families, who have been increasingly forced to depend on cash crop production.

The collection of aquatic animals is widely practiced by the whole community, rich and poor alike. Upland streams and channels, particularly Huai Khrai, Huai Hua Chang, and Huai Tung Tao, provide a rich diversity of fish, crustaceans, amphibians, mollusks, reptiles, and plants that are utilized in everyday life. Rice fields are another important habitat for fish and aquatic animals that is extensively exploited. In all of the surveyed households in Khun Huai Khrai, villagers reported a dependence on fishing and the collection of aquatic animals for subsistence, ranking overall as the fourth most important activity after rice farming, cash crop production, and livestock rearing. Fish and aquatic animals are particularly important in providing protein. Women and children play an active role in the collection of aquatic species from

Fish and aquatic animals are important sources of protein for poorer families.

Wetlands adjoining the stream are important sources of wild fruit
and vegetables for local villagers.

streams, channels, adjoining wetlands, and paddy fields. They are also the
principal actors engaged in the preservation of aquatic products. To meet
their subsistence needs, members of poorer families rely more heavily on
hunting, fishing, and gathering, in addition to seasonal and permanent
migration to seek out wage labor and small trade in urban areas.

Over the past decade, land use in the highlands has rapidly changed
in response to external pressure from market forces, state conservation
policies, population growth, and the rising expectations and aspirations
of the highlanders themselves. The intensification of cash crop production
in the highlands has had negative impacts on the livelihoods of poorer
families. Moreoever, it has been cogently argued that cash crop
intensification in the highlands is detrimental to the rich biodiversity of
northern Thailand. Most of the cash crops introduced are low in value
compared to the high-value opium they replaced. Intensification of these

cheap cash crops, especially cabbage, inevitably implies increasing acreage or expansion of hill farms, which in turn leads to deforestation. Increasing intensification of cash crops requires the application of ever more chemical fertilizers and pesticides, which leads to ecosystem poisoning. Finally, cash crop intensification eventually leads to increased social differentiation within villages, which in turn contributes to the erosion of traditional institutions for the management of common resources, including forests, wildlife, fish, and aquatic animals.

In the areas surrounding Huai Khrai, intensification of cash crop production has resulted in a loss of top soil during each wet season. The construction of roads for transporting cash crops to markets also contributes to increasing soil erosion in the highlands. The intensification of agriculture and use of chemicals is certain to have a negative impact on aquatic diversity and the livelihoods of poorer households. Replacement of these resources with fish farming is not a viable option, as access to suitable land for pond construction is limited. The loss of aquatic diversity is sure to have a greater impact on the poor, who are more reliant on such resources. The consequences of ecosystem poisoning and soil erosion for fisheries will inevitably include increased exploitation of wildlife and non-timber forest products, and illegal logging.

PART III
LOCAL KNOWLEDGE AND GLOBALIZATION FROM BELOW

SIX

Situated Knowledge, Located Lives: Adaptive Responses to Change

Through investigation of the rapid ecological and socioeconomic changes currently facing riparian communities in Yunnan, Laos, and northern Thailand, we have seen that environmental damage in the Mekong Basin is dramatically increasing. Fisherfolk in riparian communities concur that flow regulation has reduced flood-season peaks, changing the magnitude and extent of floodplain inundation, and land–water interactions. In certain communities such as Pak Ing, fisherfolk contend that fish breeding and migration have been disrupted as altered flow regimes fail to stimulate reproduction.

Widespread environmental problems resulting from the construction of dams, waterways, and other megaprojects in the Mekong Basin have caused significant economic impacts on local communities such as loss of fisheries, agricultural land, riverbank gardens, forests, and other means of livelihood. Many local groups are faced with decreasing income. Economic necessity in turn leads to an increase in environmental exploitation by over-fishing and timber harvesting, in addition to the social breakdown caused by migration to seek jobs and economic security in urban centers. Thus, within the context of environmental degradation, resource depletion, expansion of market mechanisms, enclosure, and centralization, we also witness a growing income disparity between urban and rural sectors, an increase in poverty, and the rapid transformation of rural communities, lifestyles, and cultural practices.

Large-scale development projects also have adverse effects on local cultures. Increased transnational cooperation in infrastructural development and freer cross-border flows of people and commercial goods are posing serious challenges to local cultures and local knowledge,

lifestyles, and subsistence practices. Consequently, riparian communities have had to find new ways to adapt their knowledge and cultural
practices to cope with changing environmental and socioeconomic
contexts.

Situated Knowledge and Local Adaptation

Local ecological knowledge is dynamic and holds the potential to
modify, shift, transform, and reshape new systems of meaning as adaptive
responses of marginal communities to change. The dynamism of local
knowledge takes place within the development context as a means of
adaptation to socioeconomic and environmental change. It signifies a
continuous process of transformation, ruptures, interruptions, and
reorganization in which local knowledge is reordered, rearranged, and
repositioned so as to provide new forms of knowledge that articulate
new historical realities.

From an ethnoecological perspective (Conklin 1954, see also
Gragson and Blount 1999), local knowledge is a repertoire of situated
experience developed in particular physical and cultural contexts from
intimate interaction between people and the environment. It is
culturally embedded in its local context and grounded in particular
territories. However, local knowledge should not be placed in
opposition to modern knowledge by employing a range of binary
concepts: local knowledge versus scientific knowledge, traditional
knowledge versus modern knowledge, and folk knowledge versus
universal knowledge. Rather, the focus on local knowledge represents a
shift away from preoccupation with the centralized, technically-
oriented solutions to development problems that have failed to improve
the prospects of most of the world's marginal peasants and small farmers.
By highlighting the possible contribution to be made by knowledge in
the hands of the marginalized poor, the local knowledge concept, as
Agrawal (1995) has rightly noted, focuses both attention and resources
on those who need them most.

The term local knowledge is used here to refer to the knowledge used by local people to survive in a changing environment. Knowledge production is a process of social negotiation involving multiple actors and complex power relations and must therefore be understood in terms of change, adaptation, and dynamism (Yos 2003a, 43). In this light, diverse social actors situate local knowledge in the process of contesting and reinterpreting knowledge. Local knowledge should, therefore, be viewed as a continuous process of change, adaptation, contestation, and coexistence, in which tradition and modern, situational and hybrid, local and global are mingled together to create a complicated social life (Nygren 1999, 269).

The ethnoecological approach, with its emphasis on local knowledge, is employed here as an important conceptual tool to understand how local communities in the Mekong Basin have learned to live within their diverse ecosystems, developing sophisticated knowledge for resource management, swidden agriculture, and fish ecology. This knowledge extends to rules and ritual practices for the management of common property, the means through which local knowledge and practices are passed down from generation to generation and incorporated into the socio-cultural characteristics of the people who live by the Mekong, and the ways in which local knowledge is reordered, rearranged, and repositioned to meet the changing needs of modern times.

Local Knowledge and Livelihood Strategies

In riparian communities, livelihood strategies incorporate a number of interdependent linkages between local people and their rivers. While fisheries, vegetable gardens, rice fields, and hill farms are the most visible components of local livelihoods and economies, other resources are less visible but also important. Many of these less visible components of local livelihoods can only be understood in the light of local environmental knowledge. Local knowledge can be divided into several interrelated categories: fish ecology and micro-ecosystems, fish species, hydrology and fish migrations, and forest management.

Fish Ecology and Micro-ecosystems

The Mekong and its tributaries form a complex hydrological system that is neither well studied nor understood by outsiders. The people living along the Mekong, however, have accumulated highly sophisticated knowledge of the complex interrelationships of the area's diverse ecosystems. Villagers in Chiang Khong, for instance, divide their complex riverine ecosystem into 11 micro-ecosystems, namely, *pha* (rocks), *kok* (deep pools near the riverbanks), *don* (sandbars or islands), *hat* (sand or pebble beaches), *rong* (dry season water channels near the riverbanks that are connected to the mainstream river), *long* (dry season water channels that are disconnected from the mainstream river), *nong* (swamps or ponds), *chaem* (the heads of rapids that make strong currents), *huai* (streams), *rimfang* (riverbanks), and *kwan* (inlets) (Thai Baan Research 2006). Many of these micro-ecosystems are vital habitats and spawning grounds for local and migratory fish, as well as important fishing sites for local fishermen. In the dry season, when the water level drops lower than five meters, for example, *kok* or deep pools near the riverbanks become important habitats for many species of fish.

Fishermen in the Mekong River Basin use a wide variety of fishing methods and fishing gear. Intimate knowledge of the complex interrelationships between diverse micro-ecosystems has led to the design of remarkably diverse types of gear, each type specially designed to catch particular species of fish in specific micro-ecosystems at particular times of the year. *Mong* (gill nets) are the most popular fishing gear and are usually set vertically in the water to trap fish. In shallow areas, fish traps such as *sai* or *chan* are used to catch fish as they forage for food. Fish barrier traps of various designs and sizes are usually used by local villagers at the end of the rainy season.

Fishing gear is improved, developed, and passed down from one generation to the next. A fisherman normally sets a number of traps then checks them from time to time as he goes about his other activities along the river. Fishing gear thus also serves as a marker of each fisherman's fishing grounds and represents established rights and property relations between community members.

In northern Laos, *mong* of various mesh sizes are repaired on a regular basis.

Fish barrier traps of various designs and sizes are used by the Tai Lue of Chiang Rung.

Chan, a drop door trap, is used to catch larger fish in the rivers.

Sai of various shapes and sizes are popular fish traps used in the Mekong Basin.

Fish Species and Migrations

Small-scale fishermen possess a vast amount of local ecological knowledge about the fish and fisheries of the Mekong and its tributaries. Villagers in Mekong riparian communities first categorize fish according to whether or not they have scales. Fish without scales are called *pla nang* or "skin fish." Most fish with scales are of the carp family. Fish without scales include *Pangasius* and *Mystus*. These fish are large and prey on smaller fish and insects. *Pla nang* tend to fetch higher prices in the market because they are large, tasty, and easy to eat because they are not bony. Local villagers possess a wealth of knowledge not only about fish and their behavior, but also about the relationship between fish migration and changes in water levels. This knowledge comes from generations of experience and observation. One reason for villagers' detailed observations of fish is the important role fish play as a natural resource in people's daily lives.

Fish migration in the Mekong River and its tributaries is probably the most important ecological factor impacting on the livelihood of local peoples, most obviously in relation to food and nutrition, but also as an important source of income. It is believed that the Mekong River is home to more than 1,700 species of fish whose migration patterns are determined by the significant variation in the conditions of the river during the dry and rainy seasons (Coates et al. 2003). According to local people in the riparian communities in which we carried out our study, the primary triggers of fish migration are changes in water levels and related factors such as rainfall, turbidity, and water color. Consequently, the main periods for fish migration occur when the water level begins to rise at the onset of the flood season, and again when the water level begins to recede at the onset of the dry season. Furthermore, the peak spawning period for most species coincides with the start of rising water levels at the onset of the flood season. In other words, the life cycles of these fish are adapted to the hydrological conditions determined by the annual flood pulse of the Mekong River.

In northern Thailand and Laos, rainy season fish migration begins when the rains start and the river water becomes cloudy. As this area contains much laterite soil, the earth is red in color. When this soil mixes with the river, the water turns to a reddish brown. Many fishermen contend that the first fish to swim upstream during the rainy season are the large fish in the carp family. After that, fish such as *pla yon* (*Pangasius macronema*) and *pla kot* (*Mystus nemurus*) enter and swim up the tributaries. "Most species of fish swim upstream," remarks Lung Saw of Ban Hat Khrai in Chiang Khong, northern Thailand. "Dozens of species of fish migrate from the Mekong to the Ing River when the rainy season begins," says Boonkong, the headman of Pak Ing village. At this time, almost all species of migratory fish carry eggs, and it is understood that the fish enter the Ing in order to spawn. "In fact, many young fish are caught in the Ing River during the rainy season. It is difficult to imagine small fish like these fighting the Mekong's current in the rainy season to enter the Ing River, so fishermen here are quite certain that spawning occurs in the flood plains of the Ing."

During the rainy season, there is a time when the water level of the Mekong rises and its flow is stronger than that of its tributaries so the tributaries can no longer flow into the Mekong's mainstream. According to Pak Ing villagers' observations, rainy season migratory fish flow along the Mekong's current and into the Ing. Local fishermen judge how far the water from the Mekong has flown into the Ing by observing the color of the water and the strength of the current. They say that many rainy season migratory fish take advantage of the change in the direction of the Mekong's current to swim into the Ing. Local fishermen contend that the same fish that swim upstream against the current at the beginning of the rainy season flow with the current into the Ing later in the season.

Wetland Fisheries

In northern Thailand and Laos, wetlands are areas that contain water for much of the year, which may or may not dry up by the end of the dry season. When the rainy season begins, wetlands are once again flooded by both rainfall and the rising waters of the Mekong and its tributaries. The most important types of wetland are ponds and *nong*, large pools of water that remain in natural depressions in the landscape after the recession of seasonal floods. During both the rainy and the dry seasons, villagers in the Ing Basin fish in the rivers and in these natural depressions. Wetland fisheries are thus an important basis of local diets and economies.

In response to growing environmental problems in the Mekong Basin and the erratic fluctuation of water levels, local communities have initiated strict management of wetland fishing grounds to conserve these fragile ecosystems, maximize the productivity of wetland fisheries, and ensure that all community members share the benefits. In the Ing Basin, local villagers employ a wide range of community-based management strategies to conserve their wetlands and floodplains. Many local communities have established conservation zones along the Ing River and other spawning grounds in the floodplains in order to protect the environment and revitalize depleted food sources. Strategies for community management of small village reservoirs include spawning habitat protection and timing control. Many local communities impose conservation measures that stipulate the type of fishing gear allowed and the timing and extent of fishing. In Phaya Mengrai, Wiang Kaen, and Thoeng districts, a great many inland swamps and ponds are managed and used according to specific environmental and socioeconomic factors.

The most common form of fisheries management in the Ing River Basin is the *nong* seasonal fishing system widely practiced in many of the basin's inland communities. Villagers in Ban San Sai Ngam, Thoeng District, for example, have in recent years imposed a year-long fishing ban on their *nong* or inland water bodies. Villagers set aside one day on which all people in the community and neighboring villages are allowed to participate in fishing activities by paying a lump sum fishing fee for each piece of fishing gear used. The day usually falls near the end of the dry season. The area is then closed to fishing again. This *nong* seasonal fishing system is designed to put off fishing until as late as possible in the

A *nong* in Ban San Sai Ngam is open for fishing by both locals and non-locals for one day a year.

dry season to provide the fish time to grow and to ensure fair and equitable distribution of the benefits of wetland fisheries among community members. This conservation-based seasonal fishing system is now commonly practiced in the Ing River Basin.

Within the context of rapid ecological change, conservation practices found in the Ing River Basin provide a clear example of how riparian communities can modify, reinterpret, and reshape their local ecological knowledge to adapt to the changing needs of modern times. In response to growing environmental problems and increasing conflicts and competition over scarce resources, local communities have adapted their ecological knowledge to establish conservation zones along the Mekong and its tributaries in order to protect their environments and revitalize depleted food sources. Mechanisms for community management of small village reservoirs, including spawning habitat protection and timing control, are being reinvented and developed to ensure the sustainable use of natural resources and fair distribution of benefits among community members.

Local Knowledge and Forest Management

The livelihood of people living in many Mekong Basin riparian communities is closely linked to the natural and community forests near their villages. These forests include the seasonally flooded riverine forests along the Mekong and its tributaries, wetland forests, hill evergreen, and semi-evergreen forests. Trees and vegetation in the immediate vicinity of riverine and wetland forests are usually flooded during the rainy season, whereas hill evergreen and semi-evergreen forests are upland forests and not subject to floods.

Large areas of seasonally flooded riverine forests can be found along the Mekong, particularly from Wiang Kaen to Luang Prabang in northern Laos, and along stretches of the Ing and other Mekong tributaries. In the Ing River Basin, many wetland or *tam* forests have been demarcated and conserved by local people as community forests. These forests are flooded as water levels increase during the rainy season, and are the habitat of a wide variety of fish, shrimp, mollusks, amphibians, reptiles, and insects, as well as larger mammals and birds. Flooded forests are crucial for maintaining a healthy aquatic ecosystem. They are the spawning grounds for many species of fish and a main source of organic nutrients. These forests also provide small fish with refuge from predators.

Much of the forest in the Mekong Basin in Laos and northern Thailand is upland forest, including hill evergreen, semi-evergreen, mixed deciduous, and dry dipterocarp forests. These forests are often managed by nearby communities and conserved as community forests. Upland forests provide communities with many essential livelihood resources. They provide the needed space for rotational hill farms for rice cultivation where paddy lands are scarce. Forests are also a prime source of food, firewood, and medicine. Local villagers collect many non-timber forest products, such as bamboo shoots, mushrooms, honey, medicinal plants, and a variety of spices, for subsistence and for sale.

Analysis of numerous examples of forest management practices in northern Thailand (Yos 2003, 169–191) suggests that local communities and ethnic groups have a deep and thorough understanding of forest resources and ecosystems, including an intimate knowledge of the microenvironments of forest and fields. The local knowledge found in these communities can contribute to better natural resource management practices and the development of more sustainable agro-ecology systems.

Local knowledge about forest management embodies four elements of understanding. First, local peoples have a deep understanding of soil, water, and forest resources in terms of agricultural production, medicine, and other aspects of practical use and, more importantly, how these natural resources are interdependent. Local people are fully aware that forests, water, and soil fertility are deeply connected; if forests are depleted, there will be no water in the streams, and this will have a serious effect on local production systems.

Second, local knowledge is situated and bound with the notion of territoriality. In practice, local people have a thorough understanding of the structure and nature of forest ecosystems. Local people are able to classify hundreds of species of trees, edible plants, medicinal herbs, and other forest products. Based on such knowledge, forests are classified into different types and customary rules and management systems are applied to each type of forest.

Third, local people have a deep understanding of forest habitats and carrying capacities. Hence different sets of rules and guidelines are established to maintain an ecological balance, such as strict rules regarding the use of watershed areas. In certain places the gathering of forest products such as mushrooms and bamboo shoots is permitted solely for domestic consumption.

The fourth element of local knowledge is related to the nutrient cycles of the tropical forest. This knowledge is clearly evident in the practice of rotational swidden agriculture. The farmer accelerates the natural decay of the forest by the burning of slashed and felled fields; the fields may then be used for a short period before being left fallow for adequate soil replenishment. By keeping field sizes small, retaining pieces of the original forest nearby for reseeding, and practicing "relic emergent" forestry (the practice of cutting back rather than uprooting certain species of valuable plants to enable quick regeneration of forest after harvest) and other management techniques that favor regeneration, forest ecosystems are sustained.

Community forests are normally classified into different types and assigned different names according to their importance and function. Based on local knowledge and traditional practices, community forests in northern Thailand can be broadly classified into three different types: *pa ton nam* "watershed catchment forests," *pa prapeni* "ceremonial forests," and *pa chai soi* "multi-purpose forests." These three types of forests are managed through local protection mechanisms and customary rules based on religious beliefs.

The preservation of *pa ton nam* watershed areas is crucial to the maintenance of local agricultural production systems and a steady water supply. In many places, surveillance teams are organized by local communities to protect the area. Even though local villagers have safeguarded watershed forests for generations, many watershed areas have now been declared state-run national parks because the government refuses to recognize local control and traditional management systems. Incongruity between local rights and national laws has resulted in increasing disputes and conflicts between government agencies and local organizations.

Pa chai soi multi-purpose forests usually cover limestone areas and are therefore unsuitable for agricultural purposes. Multi-purpose forests usually fall within the boundaries of national reserve forests, and for this reason people from other villages tend to consider them no man's land or open access areas, and are not inclined to accept local rules for conservation. This results in frequent conflicts between neighboring villages.

The environmental objectives of forest classification are to protect watershed forest, conserve flora and fauna, and maintain an ecological balance. Local knowledge about the interdependence between forests, water, and agricultural production, as well as tree species, medicinal plants, forest habitats, and carrying capacities is transferred from generation to generation. The community forestry concept also serves as a basis for the promotion of local people's sense of belonging and attachment to the community's resource base while reproducing cultural heritage.

Forest management is an integral part of local subsistence production. Community forestry is a self-initiated management system based on traditional knowledge, customs, and practices, designed to preserve watershed forests and local agro-ecosystems. Local practices of forest management are based on cultural, moral, and ecological principles, culminating in community rights. Rules, guidelines, and social organizations are established and reestablished in response to the ever-changing socioeconomic and political situations, and conflicts affecting local control over forest resources. Local people have clearly shown that they have a strong potential to manage forest resources, resolve conflicts, and disputes, and adapt their management systems to meet the changing needs of modern times. On the contrary, government agencies, particularly those concerned with environmental laws and policies, tend to be slow in adjusting to changing socioeconomic and political conditions. Contradictions in laws and policies concerning forest management and national development are the root cause of the problems surrounding sustainable resource management.

For many riparian communities, the decline of fish and aquatic resources resulting from megaprojects has led to increased pressure on forest lands. The decline in river-based production has led to increasing intensification and expansion of hill farms along riverbanks, resulting in the clearing of more and more forest lands for cash crop cultivation. In many places, forestland has declined and the forests that remain are under threat.

Forest management has been an integral part of local practices in Southeast Asia for centuries (see Saneh and Yos 1993, Hirsch 1989, 1996, Anan 2000). But as powerful demands for resources, land, and military control have guided state expansion to the furthest corners of these countries, many groups of successful forest managers have been relocated, sedentarized, victimized, and marginalized. Their local knowledge of forest ecology and forest management has been devalued and their cultures denigrated (Pathak 1995, Poulsen 2001). State-initiated large-scale development projects are thus important factors contributing to the decline of local knowledge, biodiversity, and sustainable forest management.

Local Knowledge and Bottom-Up Development

Forest and aquatic resources are two of the most important sources of nutrition and income for millions of people in the six riparian countries of the Mekong Basin. Over the past decade, increased transnational cooperation in infrastructure development and freer cross-border flows of people and commercial goods have posed serious challenges to local cultures and lifestyles, subsistence practices, local knowledge, health, and the environment. Differing sectoral interests provide many of the key resource management challenges for the Mekong Basin as a whole, as well as for individual countries. For instance, reconciling the need for the energy and foreign exchange generated by hydroelectric dams sits uneasily with biodiversity conservation and the maintenance of aquatic resources.

Forest and aquatic resources provide the bulk of the local population's protein requirements and are thus a central issue to livelihood development and a major area of risk in the disturbance of the Mekong Basin's delicate ecosystems. Sustainable forest management and cash crop production come into conflict in many parts of the Mekong Basin, and deforestation is a key threat to environmental integrity. Other key threats include the clearance of vegetation in upper watersheds, whether from illegal logging, the spread of large-scale tree plantations, or shifting cultivation; and the construction of hydroelectric dams. Current patterns of resource use and development also have different impacts on different groups. Emerging conflicts in the Mekong Basin thus arise from resource competition between different socio-political actors.

There is a need to incorporate a bottom-up planning process in the development of the Mekong Basin. Stakeholder approaches to development based on full recognition of the value of local knowledge provide an underlying framework for inclusiveness and participation, taking into consideration also the unequal political, social, and economic power structures in and between the countries involved. This new development paradigm must be adopted in future approaches to resource management in the region.

The decline of fish and aquatic resources has led to increased pressure on land and forests. Intensification of agriculture and expansion of hill farms for increased cash crop production is common along the banks of the Mekong in Laos.

SEVEN

———

Transboundary Environmental Issues
and Transnational Civil Society

Freshwater biodiversity in Asia, according to Dudgeon (2003, 2), is in peril. Among the diverse human influences upon Asian rivers, including the Mekong and its tributaries, three main threats stand out. Firstly, degradation of drainage basins (particularly through deforestation and overgrazing) is leading to increased suspended sediment loads and extensive flooding. Excessive floodplain siltation is altering habitats, causing species to decline or disappear. The second threat—river regulation and control—has been practiced widely in the region for centuries but, with the planned development of massive projects on the Mekong and its tributaries, the potential for environmental damage has dramatically increased. Flow regulation reduces flood-season peaks, changing the magnitude and extent of floodplain inundation and land–water interactions. Fish breeding migrations are disrupted as dams block migration routes and altered flow regimes fail to stimulate reproduction. River pollution is pervasive throughout the Mekong Basin, and constitutes the third threat. Untreated sewage is a particular problem in densely populated areas, and pollution by industrial effluents and mining waste is becoming more widespread.

Together, these three threats have led to declines and range constrictions in aquatic animals and those terrestrial species associated with riparian corridors and floodplains. Reversing this trend is difficult as pollution, flow regulation, and drainage-basin degradation have non-additive detrimental effects on river ecosystems, and enhance the success of exotic invasive species. Moreover, our ability to predict the outcome of human-induced change is hampered by a lack of knowledge of species' life histories and population status of the vast majority of freshwater

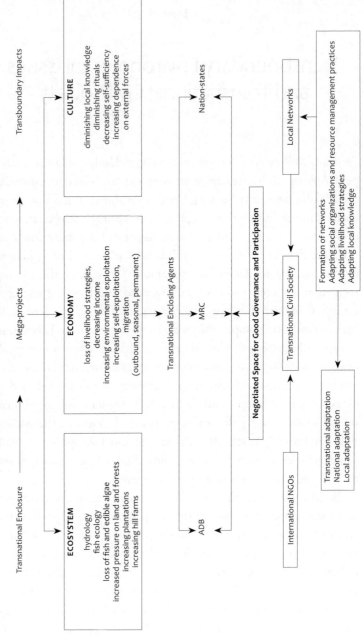

Figure 7.1 Mekong Basin Regional Development in the Global Context

species. Ecologically viable management strategies for the Mekong will succeed only if the socioeconomic context of development plans is seriously taken into account.

Transnational Enclosure and Transboundary Environmental Impacts

Over the past two decades, various countries in the Mekong Basin have tightly embraced growth-oriented development. As such, national policies have given a pre-eminent role to hydropower and irrigation projects. This trend toward technical and engineering works implies increasing state control over the management of the Mekong Basin. The absence of established public participation processes in the riparian countries also means that there is no channel at which the public can effectively influence the planning, construction, or operation of most large-scale, technology- and capital-intensive infrastructural projects. Increasing state control over the management of the Mekong Basin has resulted in the large-scale appropriation of land for the construction of dams, the loss of the region's most productive farmland and prime forests, and denial of local rights and local resource management systems, as well as widespread environmental impacts.

The negative effects of megaprojects in the Mekong Basin can be divided into three interrelated categories: impacts on ecosystems, impacts on local economies, and impacts on local cultures (see Figure 7.1). From our study of the transboundary impacts of subregional development and megaprojects on marginal communities in the Greater Mekong Subregion, especially in Yunnan, Laos, and northern Thailand, we have found that the rich biological diversity and productivity of the Mekong and its floodplains is intricately linked to the system's annual flood pulse. The rise and fall of water in the flood pulse system triggers the migration of various species of fish to spawn in the floodplains. Exchanges of water, nutrients, and organisms also occur between terrestrial and aquatic environments in the annual flood–drought cycle driven by the Mekong's hydrology that seasonally inundates flood plains

(Poulsen and Valbo-Jorgensen 2000). However, this intricate system is highly vulnerable to human-induced change, especially the control of water levels through a complex series of dams.

Large-scale water infrastructure projects in Yunnan (see Osborn 2004, 2006, 2007) have caused significant changes in the water quality, flood pulse timing, and the river's ecology as a whole. The greatest cause for concern relates to the rapid decline of fish stocks in the Mekong. Decline of fish and aquatic resources from the river is leading to increased pressure on land and forests. The intensification of agriculture and expansion of hill farms for increased cash crop production is certain to have a negative impact on the region's forests. In the areas surrounding Luang Prabang in northern Laos (Sianouvong 2000), for example, the intensification of cash crop production has caused exposed soil surfaces during the wet season, resulting in soil erosion. The construction of roads for transporting cash crops to markets also contributes to soil erosion and deforestation in the highlands. The ecological impact of mega development projects on the Mekong River will inevitably lead to increased exploitation of wildlife, non-timber forest products, and illegal logging.

The expansion of rubber plantations in Yunnan and Laos and teak plantations in Cambodia is also resulting in a rapid decline in natural forests. Tree plantations are rapidly changing the landscape throughout the Mekong Basin. Their expansion is fast and extensive, penetrating into farmlands and all too often taking the place of community forests with their inherent biological diversity. Various governments in the Mekong Basin have granted thousands upon thousands of hectares of land concessions to private companies for industrial tree plantations, with the most rapid increases in Laos and Cambodia. Granting private companies exclusive use of large tracts of forest and agricultural land has led to increasing conflicts and competition between the private sector and local peoples over natural resources. Tree plantations and their production of monoculture woodlots lead to rapid degradation of natural forests and biodiversity; the use of pesticides often causes severe pollution of local water sources. Tree plantations also have serious impacts on traditional beliefs and local forest management practices.

The widespread environmental problems resulting from the mega-projects in the Mekong Basin have led to significant economic impacts such as loss of fisheries, agricultural land, community forests, riverbank gardens, and other means of livelihood. Many local groups are faced with decreasing income. Economic necessity has led to environmental exploitation in the form of over-fishing and timber harvesting, and increased migration to seek jobs and economic security in urban centers. Large-scale development projects also have adverse effects on local cultures.The Mekong and its communities are under dire threat from external forces beyond local control.

Responses from the Grassroots

Local communities, however, are not simply passive receptors of mainstream development discourse. In addition to seeking out new livelihood strategies through urban migration and diversification of occupations, local communities are experimenting with various adaptive management approaches. In many areas, conservation is seen as critical for successful adaptive management. The ecological deterioration of the Mekong, and the resulting decline of fish stocks, *kai*, and riverbank gardens, provides an impetus for the formation of grassroots conser-vation groups and local networks to alleviate the negative impacts of development. For example, during an initial move to investigate and document the widespread environmental impacts of soil erosion and unnatural flow of the Mekong in the late 1990s, a loosely bound coalition of local and international NGOs formed the "Rak Chiang Khong" (Love Chiang Khong) group to coordinate investigative work in Chiang Khong, northern Thailand. This group later developed into an alliance between local residents, fishermen, teachers, academics, and local and international NGOs.

In an attempt to simultaneously conserve both the endangered giant catfish and the ancestral fishing traditions that formed an important

part of fishermen's way of life, the Rak Chiang Khong group successfully called for a co-management program and government-sponsored
study of the giant catfish. Furthermore, the group has successfully
demarcated conservation zones on the Mekong and local fishermen
have gradually been persuaded to stop fishing for the giant catfish. At
the same time, The *liang luang* ritual to worship the guardian spirits has
been preserved as an important part of local cultural heritage and
continues to be performed in mid-April every year.

Over the past decade, local communities affected by the transboundary
impacts of river basin development projects have witnessed a dramatic
transformation in livelihood strategies, food security, and occupations.
In response to the erratic fluctuation of water levels, various riparian
communities along the 84 kilometer stretch of the Mekong in northern
Thailand have adjusted their local knowledge of fish ecology and
resource management in order to preserve the lives of the Mekong, its
tributaries, and natural habitats, and the people whose lives are
dependent upon them. Numerous communities in Chiang Saen, Chiang
Khong, and Wiang Kaen districts have established conservation zones
and protected areas along the river. Certain communities have imposed
new conservation measures which include spawning habitat protection
and timing control. Many local communities in northern Thailand are
beginning to appreciate the need to promote conservation measures.
Consequently, conservation ethics have been promoted and widely
accepted by stakeholders that have legitimate interests in how local
resources are managed. Many local communities also recognize that the
formation of networks and institutional mechsnisms that will allow
wider stakeholder participation in resource management is essential
for successful environmental protection and resource management
strategies.

Civil society groups that are concerned about transboundary environmental issues in the Mekong Basin are often involved in supporting
local communities affected by upstream development. A fine case in
point here is the Thai Baan research project spearheaded by a group of
Thai and international civil society organizations to assist local people

in gathering information and data and voice their concerns to decision-makers. The project provides research assistants—academics, students, and NGOs—who help villagers-cum-researchers with the practicalities and logistics of conducting the research. The methods used include participatory observation, focus group discussion, in-depth interviews, validation of data by local experts, data classification, and analysis.

Thai Baan research was first implemented at the beginning of the new millennium at the site of Pak Mun Dam in northeast Thailand. Pak Mun Dam was built in 1994 by the Electricity Generating Authority of Thailand with financing from the World Bank. After a decade of resistance by local villagers, the government decided in June of 2001 to open the dam gates for one year and commissioned studies, carried out by Ubon Ratchathani University, on local fisheries, the environment, the amount of energy generated, and the dam's social impacts. At the same time, local people affected by Pak Mun, with the help of civil society groups and academics, initiated a villagers' research project, known as "*Ngan Wijai Thai Baan*" (Thai Baan Research), to investigate the effects of opening of the dam gates and to empower communities by promoting local knowledge on resource management. It was found that fisheries flourished along the Mun River and people's livelihoods began to recover once the Thai government opened the gates of the Pak Mun Dam.

The villagers-cum-researchers found that with the opening of the dam gates 156 species of fish returned to the Mun River, and 75 types of fishing gear were efficiently employed again. After the opening of the dam gates, the river was once again full of fishing boats. Traps were set along the banks of the river. Pak Mun fishermen put their situated knowledge to productive use again. The fertility of the river returned, along with the pride and dignity of the fishers. Hunger vanished from the communities of the Pak Mun. After the dam gates were opened, villagers regained access to 342 plant species that grow in the rapids and on the islands, riverbanks, and tributaries of the Mun River. These plants are utilized in many ways. No less than 138 species are used as herbal medicine and food. Some are used for fish bait, fishing gear, livestock feed, rope, timber, household appliances, and for performing rituals. The research team found 56 plant species alone that only grow in the river's rapids (Searin 2002).

Over the past five years, Thai Baan research has also been carried out in the lower Songkram River Basin, another tributary of the Mekong in northeastern Thailand, and in the Mekong River Basin in Chiang Khong and Wiang Kaen districts of northern Thailand. Thai Baan research demonstrates peoples' deep understanding of their local ecology. It also illustrates the capacity of local people to undertake a wide range of research activities and document the close relationships between local livelihoods, cultures, and complex river-based ecosystems. The research offers a way in which local people's knowledge and experience can form the cornerstone of natural resource monitoring and assessment, allowing local people to take a leading role in local sustainable development. Thai Baan research also demonstrates the importance of local participation in monitoring transboundary impacts on the Mekong and its tributaries. It illustrates the importance of comparative data regarding water quality, hydrology, and aquatic biodiversity derived from various stakeholders, especially data gained from local knowledge in addition to that of government and inter-government agencies, and international development banks.

The success of grassroots and civil society groups in their efforts to empower local communities to conduct their own conservation and natural resource management practices has been demonstrated time and again. Poffenberger and Stone (1996, 212), for example, have found that by empowering local communities to protect community forests, these forests will regenerate rapidly, yielding food items, fuel, non-timber forest products, and timber for local needs. The cost of natural regeneration is generally estimated to be one to five percent of that for establishing tree plantations. More importantly, community-based management vests rights and responsibilities locally, while plantations tend to reinforce the power of government bureaucracies and com-mercial firms.

The Formation of Transnational Civil Society in the Mekong Basin

All across the world, local groups and civil society organizations are forming networks, linking their actions and voices in new ways to challenge global power and exclusion, and to demand greater social justice and inclusion. The growing impact of cross-border civil society networks and campaigns on global regional policy has made transnational civil society an increasingly important phenomenon (Khagram, Riker, and Sikkink 2002).

Transnational civil society (TCS) refers to "self-organized advocacy groups that undertake voluntary collective action across state borders in pursuit of what they deem the wider public interest." (Price 2003, 580; see also Florini 1999, 1–3). According to Batliwala and Brown (2006, 2), it is helpful to think of TCS as a concept made up of three interrelated aspects: organizations and associations; societal values, aspirations and norms; and spheres for public discourse on critical issues.

To a great extent, TCS has a complex relationship with the globalization process. Social anthropologist Arjun Appadurai (2006, xiii–xv) warns against two equally common conceptual mistakes. The first is the tendency of some observers to see TCS as a simple and benign democratic counterpart of globalization, operating across national boundaries just as it did historically within national boundaries. In this form, TCS is seen simply as the unofficial extension of international politics and economics, a sort of democratic lubricant for official negotiations between states and corporations around the rules and norms of globalization. The second conceptual mistake is the image of TCS as wholly driven by its opposition to market-driven globalization. Anti-globalization movements have many interesting claims and objectives, but TCS is not the same as the network of movements described collectively as standing in opposition to globalization.

Contrary to the above-mentioned misconceptions, the crux of TCS is the challenge of shaping the globalization process so that it is more inclusive, more responsive, more equitable, and more ethical. Appadurai further suggests that the main purpose of TCS is to strengthen the "voice" approach to the current shape of globalization. That is, TCS is best served by "making its central project the building of a critical voice in the face of what looks like the inevitable demands of economic globalization" (Appadurai 2006, xiv). The most crucial question that is raised by "voice" as the key to TCS is how TCS can position itself in relation to nation-states in which local civil society movements remain embedded. For example, communities affected by transnational megaprojects with transboundary impacts are faced with compounded processes of marginalization, in the sense that they need to negotiate not only with their own governments, but also through their own governments with neighboring (and sometimes more powerful) state authorities. The grassroots opposition to the Upper Mekong Navigation Improvement Project is a fine case in point here.

In early 2002, villagers in Chiang Khong, northern Thailand submitted a petition to the Thai government demanding a moratorium on the Chinese-led navigation improvement project. Another petition, signed by 76 organizations from 25 countries, was submitted to Mekong governments in July 2002 calling for a halt to the project until comprehensive environmental and social impact assessments were conducted. Originally, the Upper Mekong Navigation Improvement Project (see Campbell 2003) consisted of three phases. But following concerns expressed by international civil society organizations and downstream countries about the project's adverse effects on the river's ecosystem, China agreed to limit the blasting of rapids. A Chinese delegation later informed Burma and members of the MRC (the Mekong River Commission, comprised of Thailand, Laos, Cambodia and Vietnam) that it would carry out only phase one of the project. Joern Kristensen, chief executive officer of the MRC, said the decision to scale down the blasting of the rapids resulted from concerns voiced by downstream countries over the impact of the project on the lives of people living on the river. He said that the decision was based on an Environmental Impact Assessment (EIA) prepared by Monash University's Environment

Institute in December of 2001. The EIA pointed out that the project could affect food security, cultural sites, aesthetics, and local residents' health, and disrupt existing patterns of river use. The study also questioned whether the economic benefits of the project would be distributed equally among the riparian countries. It suggested that the project should have more input from the public.

The partial success of grassroots groups in the Mekong Basin, in collaboration with institutes of higher learning and local and international NGOs, in persuading the Chinese government to terminate the navigation project is a clear example of the bargaining power of transnational civil society groups over environmental and human rights issues. Many local civil society organizations and community-based organizations have found it fruitful to work in partnership with national and international organizations to advance their agendas. It remains to be seen whether this success will lead to a major advance in efforts to build a durable transnational civil society in the Mekong Basin. Such a TCS could serve as a forum in which the voices of all stakeholders could be heard, and a negotiated space of good governance and participation in the true sense of comanagement of natural resources between local and national agencies could be realized.

Concluding Remarks

Over the past decades, initiatives that foster community participation in resource management have not been part of the mainstream development paradigm. While it is now fashionable for international donor agencies to profess their belief in the importance of participatory grassroots efforts, action on the ground still too often fails to support the rhetoric. For all their promises to implement the UN's Agenda 21, nation states tend more to pay lip service to the principle of community-based resource management than to put it into actual practice. Setting up appropriate institutional structures and legal frameworks to allow wider stakeholder participation in resource management is essential for the successful implementation of better resource management strategies.

Proposals have been made to implement co-management systems in place of previously centralized approaches. (see, for example, the more recent works of Borrini-Feyerabend 2000 and Tyler 2006). Such decentralized systems by definition involve local people in a greater degree of decision-making, resulting in more flexible management systems, with a greater likelihood of formulating and enforcing regulations that best correspond to real needs at the local level.

Amidst the rapid structural transformation taking place in the region, local people may be able to identify critical problems and to articulate initial visions for protecting the commons and creating sustainable resource management systems. A long-term solution will require wider participation and regional linkages with other stakeholders and institutions. Creating and implementing solutions for transnational problems often require local and civil society organizations to engage with policymakers, inter-government agencies, and financial institutions. The success of transnational civil activism in solving some of the critical challenges facing the Mekong River requires active support from both international and local communities in order to achieve the vision of sustainable resource management for the whole region.

Appendixes

The appendixes included here provide information on varieties of fish, fish status, fishing techniques, and bait used by local communities in the Mekong River. Data are obtained from in-depth interviews with local villagers, especially from Hat Khrai and Pak Ing villages in northern Thailand. The main purpose for including these appendixes is to provide the reader with a catalogue of Mekong fisheries according to local knowledge.

Local fishermen along the Thai-Lao border have distinguished at least ten different types of micro-ecosystems such as deep pool, sandbar, ponds, and rapids. The species listed here are selected entirely by local fishermen based on their abundance, endangerment, and commercial importance and significance in terms of local conservation.

APPENDIX 1

Fish

Kot khao, kot lueang กดขาว, กดเหลือง,
Hemibagrus filamentus

Kaban, chang yiap, ngae, kamang
กะบาล, ช้างเหยียบ, แง่, กะมัง
Puntioplites proctozysron

Kwang, takak กว่าง, ตะกาก
Cosmochilus harmandi

Kuk huean กุ๊กเฮือน
Labiobarbus leptocheila

Kang, kot kaew คัง, กดแก้ว
Hemibagrus wickioides

Kae, khayaeng hin แข้, แขยงหิน
Pseudomystus siamensis
Asian bumblebee catfish

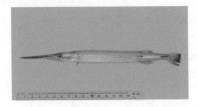

Khem, krathung heo เข็ม, กระทุงเหว
Xenantodon cancilla

Khiao kai, mu khang lai เขี้ยวไก้, หมูข้างลาย
Syncrossus helodes
Banded tiger loach, tiger botia

Kaeng แกง
Cirrhinus molitorella
Mud carp

Kaet แกต
Mystus atrifasciatus

Khae lueang แข้เหลือง
Bagarius yarrelii
Goonch

Khop, bang, khang buean ขบ, บาง, คางเบือน
Belodontichthys truncatus

Khang lai ข้างลาย
Labiobarbus leptocheila

Khiang, soi luk bua เคียง, สร้อยลูกบัว
Lobocheilus cf. *quadrilineata*

Chok sai จอกทราย
Cyclocheilichthys armatus

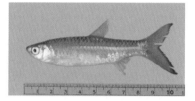

Khao ค้าว
Wallago attu
Wallago

Sio khao, sio nam khao, sio khwai
ซิวข้าว, ซิวน้ำข้าว, ซิวควาย
Rasbora tornieri Yellowtail rasbora

Sio bang, sio hua takua ซิวบาง, ซิวหัวตะกั่ว
Chela caeruleostigmata
Blue hachetfish, flying barb

Sio ao, ao ซิวอ้าว, อ้าว
Luciosoma bleekeri

Sio ao 1, mahao, nang ao
ซิวอ้าว 1, มะหาว, นางอ้าว
Raiamas guttatus
Burmese trout

Dap lao, fak phra ดาบลาว, ผักพร้า
Macrochirichthys macrochirus
Sward minnow

Taep แต๊บ
Trichogaster trichopterus
Three spot gourami

Duk na, duk dan ดุกนา, ดุกด้าน
Clarias gariepinus
North African catfish

Duk ui ดุกอุย
Clarias macrocephalus
Bighead catfish

Dut ดูด
Hypostomus plecostomus
Suckerfish, suckermouth catfish

Tong, salat ตอง, สลาด
Notopterus notopterus
Grey featherback

Tong dao, krai ตองดาว, กราย
Chitala ornata
Spotted featherback

Sai, sawai nu ทราย, สวายหนู
Helicophagus leptorhynchus

Thapthim ทับทิม
Oreochromis niloticus niloticus
Nile tilapia

Nok khao นกเขา
Osteochilus schlegelii
Giant sharkminnow

Nuan chan นวลจันทร์
Cirrhinus cirrhosus
Mrigal carp

Nin นิล
Oreochromis niloticus
Nile tilapia

Bok klet thi บอกเกล็ดถี่
Thynichthys thynnoides

Buek บึก
Pangasianodon gigas
Mekong giant catfish

Nai kham ไนคำ
Cyprinus rubrofuscus

Bok mon, bok hua mon, soi khao
บอกหม่น, บอกหัวหม่น, สร้อยขาว
Henicorhynchus siamensis
Siamese mud carp

Bok liam, hang buang บอกเหลี่ยม, หางบ่วง
Barbichthys nitidus
Sucker barb

Bok laem, soi lot บอกแหลม, สร้อยหลอด
Henicorhynchus lobatus

Pok pom, kaem cham ปกป้อม, แก้มช้ำ
Systomus orphoides
Red-cheek barb

Bu, bu sai ปู่, ปู่ทราย
Oxyeleotris marmoratus
Marble goby

Phia, ka dam เพี้ย, กาดำ
Morulius chrysophekadion
Greater black shark

Pik daeng, taphian thong ปีกแดง, ตะเพียนทอง
Barbonymus altus
Red-tailed tinfoil

Fa ong, taphap nam ฝาออง, ตะพาบน้ำ
Amyda cartilagenea
Common Asiatic softshell

Mapaep 1, paep khuai มะแปบ 1, แปบควาย
Paralaubuca harmandi

Mong yang โมงยาง
Pangasius bocourti

Mong ot, to, pho โมงออด, เต๊าะ, เผาะ
Pho Pangasius conchopilus

Mon มอน
Scaphiodonichthys acanthopterus

Mapaep, Paep มะแปบ, แปบ
Paralaubuca typus

Mang มัง
Cyclocheilichthys armatus

Man, lep mue nang มัน, เล็บมือนาง
Crossocheilus reticulatus

Man mup, kho มันมูบ, ค้อ
Schistura spp.

Mang, pik lueang, thaphian khao
มาง, ปีกเหลือง, ตะเพียนขาว
Barbonymus gonionotus

Yon, sangkawat thong khom
ยอน สังกะวาดท้องคม
Pteropangsius pleurotaenia

167

Yong lang khiao, sangkawat thong lueang
ยอนหลังเขียว, สังกะวาดเหลือง
Pangasius macronema

Waen, paen kaeo แว่น, แป้นแก้ว
Parambassis siamensis

Samok, samo สโมก, สะโม้
Miconema micronema

Sadet สะเด็ด, หมอ
Anabas testudineus

Sakang, tum สะกาง, ตุม
Puntioplites bulu

Sapak, pak nuat สะป้าก, ปากหนวด
Hypsibarbus vernayi

Sapak 1, Chat สะป้าก 1, จาด
Hypsibarbus malcolmi
Goldfin tinfoil barb

Sapak 2 สะป้าก 2, ตะพาก
Taphak Hypsibarbus wetmorei

Satup, mo thet, mo chang yiap
สะตึบ, หมอเทศ, หมอช้างเหยียบ
Pristolepis fasciatus

Sik, kasup khit สิก, กะสูบขีด
Hampala macrolepidota
Hampala barb

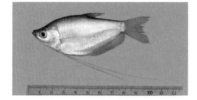

Salat, kradi nang สะลาด, กระดี่นาง
Trichogaster microlepis
Moonlight gourami

Nam fai, nam lang หนามฝ้าย, หนามหลัง
Mystacoleucus marginatus

Nam fai 1, hang lueang หนามฝ้าย 1, หางเหลือง *Mys-tacoleucus argenteus*

Wan, pik kai หวาน, ปีกไก่
Kryptopterus cheveyi

Wa mon, bua หว่ามน, บัว
Labeo dyocheilus

Hang daeng, dok ngio, soi dok ngio
หางแดง, ดอกงิ้ว, สร้อยดอกงิ้ว
Epalzeorhynchos frenatus
Rainbow sharkminnow

Lim, chon หลิม, ช่อน
Chana striata
Striped snakehead

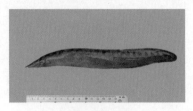

Lat, krathing หลาด, กระทิง
Mastacembelus armatus
Zig-zag eel

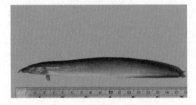

Lot, lot lang chut หลด, หลดหลังจุด
Macrognathus semiocellatus

Oen, suea เอิน, เสือ
Probarbus jullieni
Jullien's golden carp

APPENDIX 2

Fishing Equipment

Hooks and Lines

Hook and line gear for catfish, *bet khao* เบ็ดค้าว

Hang line fishing, *bet khwaen* เบ็ดแขวน

Box and line fishing, *bet klong* เบ็ดกล่อง

Hook fishing with a lure, *bet lam* เบ็ดล่าม

Bottle gourd-shaped hook fishing, *bet nam tao* เบ็ดน้ำเต้า

Surface long line fishing, *bet rao* เบ็ดราว

Pole and line fly fishing, *bet sit* เบ็ดซิด

Nets

Lift net, *cham, yo* จ้ำ, ยอ

Lift net, *sot* สอด
Triangular scoop net, *chon* ซอน

Triangular scoop net, *tuang khan* ด่วงคัน

Cast net, *hae* แห

Gill net, *hae* แห

Large long gill net, *mong lai* มองไหล

Handled scoop net, *hing* ทิ่ง

Gill net, *mong yang* มองหยั่ง

Handled scoop net, *katong* กะต่อง

Traps

Duck-shaped basket trap, *khong pet* ข้องเป็ด

Funnel basket trap, *sailan* ไซลัน

Horizontal cylinder trap, *lop* ลอบ

173

Upright basket trap, *tum* ตุ้ม

Basket eel trap, *tum ian* ตุ้มเอียน

Bamboo tube trap, *katam* กะต้ม

Plunge basket, *sum* สุ่ม

APPENDIX 3

Fish Bait

Cricket, leaping chirping insect, *ching kung* จิ้งกุ่ง

Kind of local cricket, *maeng i niao* แมงอีเนี่ยว

Kind of local insect, *maeng mai* แมงมาย

Moth, *maeng mao* แมงเม่า

Red ant, *mot daeng* มดแดง

Earthworm, *sai duean suan* ไส้เดือนสวน

Kind of worm, *maeng mae* แมงแม้

Prawn, *kung* กุ้ง

Fingerling, *pla yuea* ปลาเหยื่อ

Preserved fish, *pla ra* ปลาร้า

Fig, *phon maduea suk* ผลมะเดื่อสุก

APPENDIX 4 Fish, Conservation Status, Fishing Techniques, and Bait (by location)

Table 1 Hat Khrai in the Mekong River Ecosystem

No.	Local name	Scientific name/ Common name	Status	Fishing technique	Bait
1	Bok, hua mon บอก, หัวหม่น	*Henicorhynchus siamensis* Siamese mud carp	Endangered	Gill net, lift net	
2	Bok khang lai บอกข้างลาย	*Dangila siamensis*	Endangered	Gill net, lift net	
3	Bu บู่	*Oxyeleotris marmorata* Marble goby	Endangered	Gill net, cast net funnel basket trap	
4	Buek บึก	*Pangasianodon gigas* Mekong giant catfish	Extinct	Gill net, lift net, hand operated drift net	
5	Dang daeng ดังแดง	*Hemisilurus mekongensis*	Endangered	Gill net, hook and line gear	Fingerling, weevil, small prawn, ant, worm
6	Dok ngio ดอกงิ้ว	*Epalzeorhynchos frenatus* Rainbow sharkminnow	Endangered	Gill net	
7	Duk ui ดุกอุย	*Clarias macrocephalus* Bighead catfish	Endangered	Gill net, cast net, hook and line gear	Worm
8	Fa mai ฟ้าไม	*Amphothistes laosensis*	Endangered	Gill net, surface long line fishing	
9	Huem ฮืม	*Crossochellus delacouri*	Endangered	Gill net, hook and line gear	
10	Ka ก๊ะ	*Tor tambroides* Thai mahseer	Endangered		
11	Kaeng แกง	*Cirrhinus molitorella* Mud carp	Endangered	Gill net, funnel basket trap, cast net	
12	Kaet แกต	*Mystus atrifasciatus*	Endangered	Gill net, cast net, hook fishing with a lure, hook and line gear	Preserved fish, worm, insect
13	Kang คั่ง	*Hemibagrus wickioides*	Endangered	Gill net, cast net, funnel basket trap, hook and line gear	Worm, fingerling, insect
14	Khae dam แข้ดำ	*Bagarius bagarius* Goonch	Endangered	Gill net, cast net, hook and line gear	Fingerling, ant, moth, worm
15	Khae lueang แข้เหลือง	*Bagarius yarrelli* Goonch	Endangered	Gill net, cast net, hook and line gear	Fingerling, ant, moth, worm

177

Table 1 Hat Khrai in the Mekong River Ecosystem (cont.)

16	Khao ฅาว	*Wallago attu* Goonch		Hook and line gear, gill net	Fingerling, weevil, small prawn
17	Khem เข็ม	*Xenentodon cancilla*	Endangered	Lift net, handled scoop net	
18	Khiao kai เขียวไก่	*Syncrossus helodes* Banded tiger loach, tiger botia	Endangered	Gill net, cast net	
19	Kot dam กดดำ	*Hemibagrus* sp. Baung jaksa, crystal-eyed catfish	Endangered	Gill net, hook and line gear	Worm, small prawn, and weevil, ant, or other insects
20	Kot lueang กดเหลือง	*Hemibagrus filamentus*	Endangered	Gill net, hook and line gear	Worm, small prawn, weevil, ant, or other insects
21	Kuan ก้วน	*Channa marulia* Giant snakehead	Endangered	Gill net, hook and line gear	Worm, small prawn, fingerling
22	Kwang กว้าง	*Cosmochilus harmandi*	Endangered	Gill net	
23	Lat หลาด	*Mastacembelus armatus* Zig-zag eel	Endangered	Hook and line gear	Worm
24	Lim หลิม	*Channa striata* Striped snakehead, snakehead murrel	Endangered	Gill net, cast net, hook and line gear	Fingerling, small prawn, worm
25	Loem เลิ่ม	*Pangasius sanitwongsei* Chao Phraya giant catfish	Extinct	Hand-operated drift net, big hook and line gear	Fingerling, fermented bait, rotten stuff
26	Mahao มะขาว	*Raiamas guttatus* Burmese trout	Endangered	Gill net	
27	Man khom มันขม	*Garra fascicauda*	Endangered	Gill net, cast net, lift net	
28	Man mut มันมุด	*Gyrinocheilus pennocki* Spotted algae eater	Endangered	Gill net, cast net	
29	Mang มาง	*Sikukia gudgeri*	Endangered	Gill net, cast net	
30	Mapaep มะแปบ	*Paralaubuca harmandi*	Endangered	Gill net, cast net, lift net	
31	Mong yang โมงยาง	*Pangasius bocourti*	Endangered	Gill net, hook and line gear	Fig
32	Nai kham ในคำ	*Cyprinus rubrofuscus*	Endangered	Gill net	
33	Nin นิล	*Oreochromis niloticus* Nile tilapia	Endangered	Gill net	
34	Nuan chan นวลจันทร์	*Cirrhinus crihorus* Mrigal carp	Endangered	Gill net	

Table 1 Hat Khrai in the Mekong River Ecosystem (cont.)

	Local name	Scientific name / Common name	Conservation status	Fishing techniques	Bait
35	Pao เป้า	Monotrete turgidus / Brown puffer	Endangered	Gill net	
36	Phia เพีย	Morulius chrysophekadion / Greater black shark	Endangered	Gill net, cast net, funnel basket trap	
37	Pik daeng ปีกแดง	Barbonymus altus / Red-tailed tinfoil	Endangered	Gill net, cast net, hook and line gear	Moth, worm, insect
38	Pik lueang ปีกเหลือง	Barbonymus gonionotus / Silver barb	Endangered	Gill net, large long gill net, cast net	
39	Salak สะลาก	Trichogaster microlepis / Midnight gourami	Endangered	Gill net, cast net, lift net	
40	Samo สะโม	Miconema micronema	Endangered	Gill net, hook and line gear	Fingerling, small prawn, worm
41	Sapak สะปาก	Hypsibarbus vernayi	Endangered	Gill net, cast net, funnel basket trap	
42	Sawai สวาย	Pangasianodon hypophthalmus / Striped catfish	Endangered	Gill net	
43	Sio ao ซิวอ้าว	Luciosoma bleekeri	Endangered	Gill net, cast net	
44	Sio nam khao ซิวน้ำข้าว	Rasbora septemtrionalis	Endangered	Gill net, handled scoop net, lift net	
45	Sio nuat ซิวหนวด	Esomus metalicus	Endangered	Gill net, lift net, handled scoop net, cast net	
46	Soi สร้อย	Henicorhynchus spp.	Endangered	Gill net, cast net, lift net	
47	Suea เสือ	Probarbus jullieni / Jullien's golden carp	Extinct	Gill net, triangular scoop net	
48	To, mong ot เต๊าะ, โมงอด	Pangasius conchophilus	Endangered	Gill net, lift net, hook and line gear	Fig
49	Tong ตอง	Notopterus notopterus / Grey featherback	Endangered	Gill net, cast net	
50	Tong dao ตองดาว	Chitala ornate / Spotted featherback	Endangered	Funnel basket trap, cast net	
51	Wa หวา	Labeo yunnanensis	Endangered	Gill net	
52	Wan หวาน	Kryptopterus cheveyi	Endangered	Gill net	Moth, worm, insect
53	Yon ยอน	Pangasius macronema	Endangered	Gill net, hook and line gear	Moth, worm, insect

180

Table 2 Khun Huai Khrai in the Upstream Mekong River Ecosystem

No.	Local name	Scientific name/ Common name	Status	Fishing technique	Bait
1	Che bua, che kloe เช่บัว, เช่กลอ	*Macrognathus siamensis* Peacock eel	Endangered	Cast net, scoop net	
2	Che chai tang, che lu cheng เช่ไจทั่ง, เช่ลู่เชิง	*Opsarius pulchellus*	Endangered	Cast net, hook and line gear	Bamboo worm
3	Che choe, che nang เช่เชอะ, เช่นั่ง	*Monopterus albus* Swamp eel	Endangered	Knife	
4	Che kang เช่กั่ง	*Channa gachua* Red-tailed snakehead	Endangered	Hook and line gear, hang line fishing, cast net, bow	Earthworm, bamboo worm, cricket
5	Che klao เช่เกลา		Endangered	Bow, hook and line gear,	Bamboo worm
6	Che kwa-a เช่ก๋วาอะ	*Garra cambodgiensis* Stonelapping minnow	Endangered	Cast net, scoop net	
7	Che leng เช่เหล่ง	*Schistura desmotes*	Endangered	Hook and line gear, cast net	Bamboo worm
8	Che nang chai เช่นั่งไจ, ปลาไหลลลาย		Extinct	Knife	
9	Che nong tao เช่นองเต๊า		Endangered	Cast net, scoop net	
10	Che pa pao เช่ป่าเป๊า		Endangered	Scoop net	
11	Che pua kang poe ye 1 เช่ปั๋วกั่งโปะเย 1		Endangered	Cast net, scoop net	
12	Che pua kang poe ye 2 เช่ปั๋วกั่งโปะเย 2	*Glyphthorax trilineatus* Three-lined catfish	Endangered	Cast net, scoop net	
13	Pla duk ปลาดุก	*Clarias gariepinus* North African catfish	Endangered	Knife	

Table 3.1 Mekong River (general)

No.	Local name	Scientific name/ Common name	Status	Fishing technique	Bait
1	Fa ong ผ้าอ้อง	Amyda cartilagenea Common Asiatic softshell	Extinct	Funnel basket trap	
2	Ian, Iai เอี่ยน, ไหล	Monopterus albus Asian swamp eel	Endangered	Basket eel trap	Rotten crab, rotten prawn
3	Kang คัง	Hemibagrus wickioides	Endangered	Gill net, hook and line gear, pole and line fly fishing, hang line fishing, cast net	Earthworm, fingerling, insect
4	Kang คัง	Channa gachua Red-tailed snakehead	Endangered	Gill net, cast net	Earthworm
5	Khae kham แข้คำ	Bagarius bagarius Goonch	Endangered	Gill net, hook and line gear, pole and line fly fishing, hang line fishing, bamboo tube trap, basket trap, triangular scoop net	Fingerling, insect, ant
6	Khae lueang แข้เหลือง	Bagarius yarrelli Goonch	Endangered	Gill net, hook and line gear, pole and line fly fishing, hang line fishing, bamboo tube trap, basket trap, triangular scoop net	Fingerling, insect, ant
7	Lim หลิม	Channa striata Striped snakehead, snakehead murrel	Endangered	Hook and line gear, lift net	Fingerling, earthworm
8	Phia เพี้ย	Morulius chrysophekadion Greater black shark	Endangered	Gill net, cast net, funnel basket trap, lift net, scoop net	
9	Rak kluai รากกล้วย	Acantopsis spp.	Endangered	Handled scoop net, lift net	
10	Salat สะลาด	Trichogaster microlepis Moonlight gourami	Endangered	Hook and line gear, lift net	
11	Taep แต๊บ	Trichogaster trichopterus Three spot gourami	Endangered	Gill net, cast net, handled scoop net	

182

Table 3.2 *Pha* (ผา): Isle Micro-ecosystem of the Mekong River

No.	Local name	Scientific name/ Common name	Status	Fishing technique	Bait
1	Kang ก้ง	*Hemibagrus wickioides*	Endangered	Hang line fishing, scoop net, cast net	Earthworm, fingerling, insect
2	Khae kham แข้คำ	*Bagarius bagarius* Goonch	Endangered	Hang line fishing, scoop net, cast net	Fingerling, ant, moth, various insects
3	Khae lueang แข้เหลือง	*Bagarius yarrelli* Goonch	Endangered	Hang line fishing, hook fishing with a lure, scoop net, cast net	Fingerling, ant, moth, various insects
4	Khao ค้าว	*Wallago attu* Wallago	Endangered	Hang line fishing, scoop net, surface long line fishing	Fingerling, weevil
5	Mapaep หมะแบบ	*Paralaubuca typus*	Endangered	Lift net, cast net, gill net	Preserved fish, cooked rice
6	Mapaep หมะแบบ 1	*Paralaubuca harmandi*	Endangered	Lift net, cast net, gill net	Preserved fish, cooked rice
7	Phia เพีย	*Morulius chrysophekadion* Greater black shark	Endangered	Lift net, triangular scoop net gill net, cast net	
8	Samok สโมก	*Micronema micronema*	Endangered	Hang line fishing, scoop net, surface long line fishing	Fingerling
9	Yon ยอน	*Pteropangsius pleurotaenia*	Endangered	Gill net	Moth, ant, earthworm, insect, dragonfly
10	Yon lang khiao ยอนหลังเขียว	*Pangasius macronema*	Endangered	Gill net	Moth, ant, earthworm, dragonfly, various insects
11	Yon lang khiao ยอนหลังเขียว 1	*Clupisoma sinensis*	Endangered	Gill net	Moth, ant, earthworm, dragonfly, various insects

Table 3.3 Khok (ดก): Deep Pool Micro-ecosystem of the Mekong River

No.	Local name	Scientific name/ Common name	Status	Fishing technique	Bait
1	Buek ปีก	Pangasianodon gigas Mekong giant catfish	Extinct	Gill net, cast net	
2	Chok sai จอกทราย	Cyclocheilichthys armatus	Endangered	Gill net, cast net	
3	Dang daeng ดังแดง	Hemisilurus mekongensis	Endangered	Gill net, triangular scoop net	
4	Kaeng แกง	Cirrhinus molitorella Mud carp	Endangered	Gill net, cast net, pole and line fly fishing, funnel basket trap	Preserved fish
5	Kang คัง	Hemibagrus wickioides	Endangered	Gill net, hang line fishing, hook and line gear, cast net	Earthworm, fingerling, various insects
6	Khae kham แข้คำ	Bagarius bagarius Goonch	Endangered	Gill net, hang line fishing, hook and line gear, hook fishing with a lure	Fingerling, ant, moth, various insects
7	Khae lueang แข้เหลือง	Bagarius yarrelii Goonch	Endangered	Gill net, hang line fishing, hook and line gear, hook fishing with a lure	Fingerling, ant, moth, various insects
8	Khao คาว	Wallago attu Wallago	Endangered	Gill net, hang line fishing, hook and line gear, hook fishing with a lure, funnel basket trap	Fingerling, weevil
9	Mang มาง	Barbonymus gonionotus Silver barb	Endangered	Gill net	
10	Mapaep มะแปบ	Paralaubuca typus	Endangered	Gill net, cast net, lift net, pole and line fly fishing	Preserved fish, cooked rice
11	Mapaep 1 มะแปบ 1	Paralaubuca harmandi	Endangered	Gill net, cast net, lift net, pole and line fly fishing	Preserved fish, cooked rice
12	Mong ot โมงออด	Pangasius conchopilus	Endangered	Gill net, bottle gourd-shaped hook fishing	Fig
13	Mong yang โมงยาง	Pangasius bocourti	Endangered	Gill net, bottle gourd-shaped hook fishing	Fig
14	Oen เอิน	Probarbus jullieni Jullien's golden carp	Extinct	Gill net, cast net	
15	Phia เพียะ	Morulius chrysophekadion Greater black shark	Endangered	Gill net, cast net, funnel basket trap, lift net, scoop net	

Table 3.3 Khok (คก): Deep Pool Micro-ecosystem of the Mekong River (cont.)

16	Salat ฉะหลาด	*Trichogaster microlepis* Moonlight gourami	Endangered	Hook and line gear, lift net	
17	Samok สโมก	*Miconema micronema*	Endangered	Gill net, hang line fishing, hook and line gear, funnel basket trap	Fingerling
18	Sik สิก	*Hampala macrolepidota* Hampala barb	Endangered	Gill net, cast net, lift net	
19	Wa หว่า	*Labeo yunnanensis*	Endangered	Gill net, cast net, lift net	
20	Wa mon หว้ามน	*Labeo dyocheilus*	Endangered	Gill net, cast net, lift net	
21	Wan หว้าน	*Kryptopterus cheveyi*	Endangered	Gill net, hook and line gear	Earthworm, moth, ant, dragonfly, various insects
22	Yon ยอน	*Pteropangsius pleurotaenia*	Endangered	Gill net, hook and line gear, pole and line fly fishing	Earthworm, moth, ant, dragonfly, various insects
23	Yon lang khiao ยอนหลังเขียว	*Pangasius macronema*	Endangered	Gill net, hook and line gear, pole and line fly fishing	Earthworm, moth, ant, dragonfly, various insects
24	Yon lang khiao ยอนหลังเขียว 1	*Clupisoma sinensis*	Endangered	Gill net, hook and line gear, pole and line fly fishing	Earthworm, moth, ant, dragonfly, various insects

Table 3.4 Don (ดอน): Sandbar Micro-ecosystem of the Mekong River

No.	Local name	Scientific name/ Common name	Status	Fishing technique	Bait
1	Bok บอก	Henicorhynchus sp.	Endangered	Gill net, lift net	
2	Bok klet thi บอกเกล็ดถี่	Thynichthys thynnoides	Endangered	Gill net, lift net	
3	Bok laem บอกแหลม	Henicorhynchus lobatus	Endangered	Gill net, lift net	
4	Bok liam บอกเหลี่ยม	Barbichthys nitidus Sucker barb	Endangered	Gill net, lift net	
5	Bok mon บอกมน	Henicorhynchus siamensis Siamese mud carp	Endangered	Gill net, lift net	
6	Bok soi บอกสร้อย	Henicorhynchus spp.	Endangered	Gill net, lift net	
7	Chok sai จอกทราย	Cyclocheilichthys armatus	Endangered	Gill net	
8	Kaet, Khayaeng แกด, แขยง	Mystus atrifasciatus	Endangered	Gill net, pole and line fly fishing	Preserved fish, insect
9	Kang คัง	Hemibagrus wickioides	Endangered	Gill net, lift net, cast net, scoop net, hook and line gear	Earthworm, fingerling, insect
10	Khae kham แข้คำ	Bagarius bagarius Goonch	Endangered	Gill net, pole and line fly fishing, hang line fishing, bamboo tube trap, basket trap, scoop net	Fingerling, ant, moth, insect
11	Khae lueang แข้เหลือง	Bagarius yarrelli Goonch	Endangered	Gill net, pole and line fly fishing, hang line fishing, bamboo tube trap, basket trap, scoop net	Fingerling, ant, moth, insect
12	Khao ค้าว	Wallago attu Wallago	Endangered	Gill net, pole and line fly fishing, hang line fishing, funnel basket trap, scoop net	Fingerling, weevil
13	Kot dam กดดำ	Hemibagrus wickii Baung jaksa, crystal-eyed catfish	Endangered	Gill net, pole and line fly fishing, hang line fishing, scoop net, cast net, basket trap	Earthworm, small prawn, preserved fish, moth, ant, various insects
14	Kot khao กดขาว	Hemibagrus filamentus	Endangered	Gill net, pole and line fly fishing, hang line fishing, scoop net, cast net, basket trap	Earthworm, small prawn, preserved fish, moth, ant, various insects

Table 3.4 Don (ดอน): Sandbar Micro-ecosystem of the Mekong River (cont.)

	Local name	Scientific name	Status	Fishing gear	Bait
15	Kwang กว้าง	Cosmochilus harmandi	Endangered	Gill net, lift net, cast net, funnel basket trap	
16	Phia เพี้ย	Morulius chrysophekadion Greater black shark	Endangered	Gill net, lift net, cast net, funnel basket trap, scoop net	
17	Sik สิก	Hampala macrolepidota Hampala barb	Endangered	Gill net	
18	Wan หว่าน	Kryptopterus cheveyi	Endangered	Gill net, hook and line gear	Moth, ant, dragonfly, various insects
19	Yon ยอน	Pteropangsius pleurotaenia	Endangered	Gill net, hook and line gear, pole and line fly fishing	Moth, ant, earthworm, dragonfly, various insects
20	Yon lang khiao ยอนหลังเขียว	Pangasius macronema	Endangered	Gill net, hook and line gear, pole and line fly fishing	Moth, ant, earthworm, dragonfly, various insects
21	Yon lang khiao ยอนหลังเขียว 1	Clupisoma sinensis	Endangered	Gill net, hook and line gear, pole and line fly fishing	Moth, ant, earthworm, dragonfly, various insects

Table 3.5 *Hat* (หาด): Sand Beach Micro-ecosystem of the Mekong River

No.	Local name	Scientific name/ Common name	Status	Fishing technique	Bait
1	Bok บอก	*Henicorhynchus* sp.	Endangered	Gill net, lift net	
2	Bok klet thi บอกเกล็ดถี่	*Thynichthys thynnoides*	Endangered	Gill net, lift net	
3	Bok laem บอกแหลม	*Henicorhynchus lobatus*	Endangered	Gill net, lift net	
4	Bok liam บอกเหลี่ยม	*Barbichthys nitidus* Sucker barb	Endangered	Gill net, lift net	
5	Bok mon บอกมน	*Henicorhynchus siammensis* Siamese mud carp	Endangered	Gill net, lift net	
6	Bok soi บอกซ้อย	*Henicorhynchus* spp.	Endangered	Gill net, lift net	
7	Kaeng แกง	*Cirrhinus molitorella* Mud carp	Endangered	Gill net, cast net, lift net, hook and line gear, funnel basket trap	Preserved fish
8	Kang กั้ง	*Hemibagrus wickioides*	Endangered	Gill net, cast net,scoop net,	Earthworm, fingerling, insect
9	Khae kham แข้คำ	*Bagarius bagarius* Goonch	Endangered	Gill net, hook and line gear, bamboo tube trap, basket trap	Earthworm, fingerling, ant, various insects
10	Khae lueang แข้เหลือง	*Bagarius yarrelli* Goonch	Endangered	Gill net, cast net, lift net, hook and line gear, funnel basket trap, bamboo tube trap	Fingerling, ant, various insects
11	Khiao kai เขียวไก่	*Syncrossus helodes* Banded tiger loach, tiger botia	Endangered	Gill net, lift net	
12	Man มัน	*Crossocheilus reticulatus*	Endangered	Gill net, cast net	
13	Mapaep มะแปบ	*Paralaubuca typus*	Endangered	Gill net, lift net, hook and line gear, pole and line fly fishing	Preserved fish, cooked rice
14	Mapaep 1 มะแปบ 1	*Paralaubuca harmandi*	Endangered	Gill net, lift net, hook and line gear	Preserved fish, cooked rice
15	Nam fai หนามไฟ	*Mystacoleucus marginatus*	Endangered	Gill net, hook and line gear, pole and line fly fishing	Moth
16	Nam fai 1 หนามไฟ 1	*Mystacoleucus argenteus*	Endangered	Gill net, hook and line gear, pole and line fly fishing	Moth
17	Sio ao 1 ซิวอ้าว 1	*Raiamas guttatus* Burmese trout	Endangered	Gill net	
18	Wa ว่า	*Labeo yunnanensis*	Endangered	Gill net, cast net, lift net	
19	Wa mon ว่ามน	*Labeo dyocheilus*	Endangered	Gill net, cast net, lift net	

188

Table 3.6 Rong (ร้อง): Watercourse Micro-ecosystem of the Mekong River

No.	Local name	Scientific name/ Common name	Status	Fishing technique	Bait
1	Bok บอก	Henicorhynchus sp.	Endangered	Gill net, lift net	
2	Bok klet thi บอกเกล็ดถี่	Thynichthys thynnoides	Endangered	Gill net, lift net	
3	Bok laem บอกแหลม	Henicorhynchus lobatus	Endangered	Gill net, lift net	
4	Bok liam บอกเหลี่ยม	Barbichthys nitidus Sucker barb	Endangered	Gill net, lift net	
5	Bok mon บอกมน	Henicorhynchus siammensis Siamese mud carp	Endangered	Gill net, lift net	
6	Bok soi บอกสร้อย	Henicorhynchus spp.	Endangered	Gill net, lift net	
7	Sio bang ซิวบาง	Chela caeruleostigmata Blue hachetfish, flying barb	Endangered	Handled scoop net, gill net	
8	Sio khao ซิวข้าว	Rasbora tornieri Yellowtail rasbora	Endangered	Handled scoop net, gill net	
9	Wan หวาน	Kryptopterus cheveyi	Endangered	Gill net, lift net, pole and line fly fishing	Moth, dragonfly, various insects
10	Yon ยอน	Pteropangsius pleurotaenia	Endangered	Gill net, lift net, hook and line gear, pole and line fly fishing	Moth, ant, earthworm, dragonfly, various insects
11	Yon lang khiao ยอนหลังเขียว	Pangasius macronema	Endangered	Gill net, lift net, hook and line gear, pole and line fly fishing	Moth, ant, earthworm, dragonfly, various insects
12	Yon lang khiao 1 ยอนหลังเขียว 1	Clupisoma sinensis	Endangered	Gill net, lift net, hook and line gear, pole and line fly fishing	Moth, ant, earthworm, dragonfly, various insects

Table 3.7 Chaem (แจ่ม): Rapids Micro-ecosystem of the Mekong River

No.	Local name	Scientific name/ Common name	Status	Fishing technique	Bait
1	Dang daeng ดังแดง	Hemisilurus mekongensis	Endangered	Cast net, scoop net, lift net	
2	Kaeng แกง	Cirrhinus molitorella Mud carp	Endangered	Cast net, scoop net, lift net	
3	Kang คัง	Hemibagrus wickioides	Endangered	Cast net, scoop net, lift net	
4	Khae kham แข้คำ	Bagarius bagarius Goonch	Endangered	Cast net, scoop net, lift net	
5	Khae lueang แข้เหลือง	Bagarius yarrelii Goonch	Endangered	Cast net, scoop net, lift net	
6	Nai kham ไนคำ	Cyprinus rubrofuscus	Endangered	Cast net, scoop net, lift net	
7	Phia เพีย	Morulius chrysophekadion Greater black shark	Endangered	Cast net, scoop net, lift net	
8	Samok สัมก	Miconema micronema	Endangered	Cast net, scoop net, lift net	Fingerling

Table 3.8 Nong (หนอง): Pond Micro-ecosystem of the Mekong River

No.	Local name	Scientific name/ Common name	Status	Fishing technique	Bait
1	Bok บอก	*Henicorhynchus* sp.	Endangered	Gill net, cast net, lift net	
2	Bok klet thi บอกเกล็ดถี่	*Thynichthys thynnoides*	Endangered	Gill net, cast net, lift net	
3	Bok laem บอกแหลม	*Henicorhynchus lobatus*	Endangered	Gill net, cast net, lift net	
4	Bok liam บอกเหลี่ยม	*Barbichthys nitidus* Sucker barb	Endangered	Gill net, cast net, lift net	
5	Bok mon บอกมน	*Henicorhynchus siammensis* Siamese mud carp	Endangered	Gill net, cast net, lift net	
6	Bok soi บอกซ้อย	*Henicorhynchus* spp.	Endangered	Gill net, cast net, lift net	
7	Lim หลิม	*Channa striata* Striped snakehead, snakehead murrel	Endangered	Hook and line gear, cast net	Earthworm, fingerling
8	Nin นิล	*Oreochromis niloticus* Nile tilapia	Endangered	Gill net, cast net	
9	Sio ao ซิวอ้าว	*Luciosoma bleekeri*	Endangered	Handled scoop net, gill net, cast net	
10	Sio bang ซิวบาง	*Chela caeruleostigmata* Blue hachetfish, flying barb	Endangered	Handled scoop net, gill net, cast net	
11	Thapthim ทับทิม	*Oreochromis niloticus niloticus* Nile tilapia	Endangered	Gill net, cast net	

Table 3.9 *Rim Fang* (ริมฝั่ง): Riverbank Micro-ecosystem of the Mekong River

No.	Local name	Scientific name/ Common name	Status	Fishing technique	Bait
1	Bok บอก	*Henicorhynchus* sp.	Endangered	Gill net, lift net	
2	Bok klet thi บอกเกล็ดถี่	*Thynichthys thymnoides*	Endangered	Gill net, lift net	
3	Bok laem บอกแหลม	*Henicorhynchus lobatus*	Endangered	Gill net, lift net	
4	Bok liam บอกเหลี่ยม	*Barbichthys nitidus* Sucker barb	Endangered	Gill net, lift net	
5	Bok mon บอกมน	*Henicorhynchus siammensis* Siamese mud carp	Endangered	Gill net, lift net	
6	Bok soi บอกสร้อย	*Henicorhynchus* spp.	Endangered	Gill net, lift net	
7	Kaeng แกง	*Cirrhinus molitorella* Mud carp	Endangered	Gill net, hook and line gear, pole and line fly fishing, hang line fishing, cast net, scoop net, funnel basket trap	Preserved fish
8	Kang คัง	*Hemibagrus wickioides*	Endangered	Gill net, hook and line gear, pole and line fly fishing, hang line fishing, cast net, scoop net	Earthworm, fingerling, insect
9	Khae kham แค้ดำ	*Bagarius bagarius* Goonch	Endangered	Gill net, hook and line gear, pole and line fly fishing, hang line fishing, scoop net, bamboo tube trap, funnel basket trap	Fingerling, ant, moth, insect
10	Khae lueang แค้เหลือง	*Bagarius yarrelli* Goonch	Endangered	Gill net, hook and line gear, pole and line fly fishing, hang line fishing, scoop net, bamboo tube trap, basket trap	Fingerling, ant, moth, insect
11	Khao ค้าว	*Wallago attu* Wallago	Endangered	Gill net, hook and line gear, pole and line fly fishing, funnel basket trap, scoop net	Fingerling, weevil
12	Man mup มันมุบ	*Schistura* spp.	Endangered	Lift net	
13	Mapaep ผะแปบ	*Paralaubuca typus*	Endangered	Gill net, lift net, hook and line gear, pole and line fly fishing	Preserved fish, cooked rice
14	Mapaep 1 ผะแปบ 1	*Paralaubuca harmandi*	Endangered	Gill net, lift net, hook and line gear, pole and line fly fishing	Preserved fish, cooked rice
15	Phia เพีย	*Morulius chrysophekadion* Greater black shark	Endangered	Gill net, lift net, cast net, funnel basket trap, scoop net	
16	Sio khao สิวข้าว	*Rasbora tornieri* Yellowtail rasbora	Endangered	Handled scoop net, gill net	
17	Waen แว่น	*Parambassis siamensis*	Endangered	Cast net, handled scoop net	
18	Wan หวาน	*Kryptopterus cheveyi*	Endangered	Gill net, hook and line gear	Moth, insect, dragonfly

Table 3.10 Kwan (กว๊าน): Lake Micro-ecosystem of the Mekong River

No.	Local name	Scientific name/ Common name	Status	Fishing technique	Bait
1	Bok บอก	*Henicorhynchus* sp.	Endangered	Gill net, lift net	
2	Bok kled thi บอกเกล็ดที่	*Thynichthys thynnoides*	Endangered	Gill net, lift net	
3	Bok laem บอกแหลม	*Henicorhynchus lobatus*	Endangered	Gill net, lift net	
4	Bok liam บอกเหลี่ยม	*Barbichthys nitidus* Sucker barb	Endangered	Gill net, lift net	
5	Bok mon บอกหมน	*Henicorhynchus siammensis* Siamese mud carp	Endangered	Gill net, lift net	
6	Bok soi บอกส้อย	*Henicorhynchus* spp.	Endangered	Gill net, lift net	
7	Khae kham แข้คำ	*Bagarius bagarius* Goonch	Endangered	Gill net, hook and line gear, pole and line fly fishing, scoop net, basket trap, bamboo tube trap	Fingerling, insect ant
8	Khae lueang แข้เหลือง	*Bagarius yarrelli*	Endangered	Gill net, hook and line gear, pole and line fly fishing, scoop net, cast, basket trap	Earthworm, fingerling, insect ant
9	Kang คัง	*Hemibagrus wickioides*	Endangered	Gill net, hook and line gear, pole and line fly fishing, scoop net, cast	Earthworm, fingerling, insect ant
10	Khao คาว	*Wallago attu* Wallago	Endangered	Gill net, hook and line gear, pole and line fly fishing, basket trap, scoop net	Fingerling, weevil
11	Kot kham กดคำ	*Hemibagrus wickii*	Endangered	Gill net, hook and line gear, pole and line fly fishing, basket trap, scoop net, cast net	Earthworm, prawn, weevil insect, ant, preserved fish, moth
12	Kot khao กดขาว	*Hemibagrus filamentus*	Endangered	Gill net, hook and line gear, pole and line fly fishing, funnel basket trap, scoop net scoop net, cast net	Earthworm, prawn, weevil insect, ant, preserved fish, moth
13	Mapaep หมะแบบ	*Paralaubuca typus*	Endangered	Gill net, lift net, cast net, hook and line gear, pole and line fly fishing	Preserved fish, cooked rice
14	Mapaep 1 หมะแบบ 1	*Paralaubuca harmandi*	Endangered	Gill net, lift net, cast net, hook and line gear, pole and line fly fishing	Preserved fish, cooked rice
15	Phia เพี้ย	*Morulius chrysophekadion* Greater black shark	Endangered	Gill net, lift net, cast net, funnel basket trap	

Table 3.10 *Kwan* (กว๊าน): Lake Micro-ecosystem of the Mekong River (cont.)

16	Samok สโมก	*Miconema micronema*	Endangered	Gill net, hook and line gear, pole and line fly fishing, scoop net, funnel basket trap	Fingerling
17	Wan หวาน	*Kryptopterus cheveyi*	Endangered	Gill net, hook and line gear	Insect, dragonfly
18	Yon ยอน	*Pteropangsius pleurotaenia*	Endangered	Gill net, lift net, hook and line gear, pole and line fly fishing	Moth, ant, earthworm, insect, dragonfly
19	Yon lang khiao ยอนหลังเขียว	*Pangasius macronema*	Endangered	Gill net, hook and line gear, pole and line fly fishing	Moth, ant, earthworm, insect, dragonfly
20	Yon lang khiao 1 ยอนหลังเขียว 1	*Clupisoma sinensis*	Endangered	Gill net, hook and line gear, pole and line fly fishing	Moth, ant, earthworm, insect, dragonfly

Table 3.11 Long (หลง): Still Water Micro-ecosystem of the Mekong River

No.	Local name	Scientific name / Common name	Status	Fishing technique	Bait
1	Bok บอก	Henicorhynchus sp.	Endangered	Gill net, hook and line gear, handled scoop net, lift net	
2	Bok klet thi บอกเกล็ดที	Thynichthys thynnoides	Endangered	Gill net, hook and line gear, handled scoop net, lift net	
3	Bok laem บอกแหลม	Henicorhynchus lobatus	Endangered	Gill net, hook and line gear, handled scoop net, lift net	
4	Bok liam บอกเหลี่ยม	Barbichthys nitidus Sucker barb	Endangered	Gill net, hook and line gear, handled scoop net, lift net	
5	Bok mon บอกหม่น	Henicorhynchus siammensis Siamese mud carp	Endangered	Gill net, hook and line gear, handled scoop net, lift net	
6	Bok soi บอกส้อย	Henicorhynchus spp.	Endangered	Gill net, hook and line gear, handled scoop net, lift net	
7	Kaet, Khayaeng แกด, แขยง	Mystus atrifasciatus	Endangered	Gill net, hook and line gear, handled scoop net	Preserved fish, insect

Table 4 Ing River Ecosystem

No.	Local name	Scientific name/ Common name	Status	Fishing technique	Bait
37	Bok บอก	Henicorhynchus sp.		Gill net, cast net, hook and line gear, funnel basket trap, upright basket trap	Cooked sticky rice, mixed food
28	Bok kled thi บอกเกล็ดถี่	Thynichthys thymnoides		Gill net, cast net, hook and line gear, funnel basket trap, upright basket trap	Cooked sticky rice, mixed food
29	Bok laem บอกแหลม	Henicorhynchus lobatus		Gill net, cast net, hook and line gear, upright basket trap	Cooked sticky rice, mixed food
1	Bok liam บอกเหลี่ยม	Barbichthys nitidus Sucker barb		Gill net, cast net, hook and line gear, funnel basket trap, upright basket trap	Cooked sticky rice, mixed food
2	Bok mon บอกหมน	Henicorhynchus siammensis Siamese mud carp		Gill net, cast net, hook and line gear, funnel basket trap, upright basket trap	Cooked sticky rice, mixed food
3	Bok soi บอกซ่อย	Henicorhynchus spp.		Gill net, cast net, hook and line gear, funnel basket trap, upright basket trap	Cooked sticky rice, mixed food
4	Bu บู่	Oxyeleotris Marmorata Marble goby		Gill net, cast net	
5	Buek บึก	Pangasiodon gigas Mekong giant catfish	Endangered	Gill net, cast net	
6	Chado ชะโด	Channa micropeltes Giant snakehead	Endangered	Gill net cast net, hook and line gear, funnel basket trap	Earthworm, fingerling, small toad
7	Chon sai, kho ชอนทราย, ขอ		Endangered	Scoop net	
8	Dap lao ดาบลาว	Macrochirichthys macrochirus Sward minnow	Endangered	Gill net, cast net, hook and line gear, funnel basket trap	Earthworm, silkworm
9	Duk ดุก	Clarias gariepinus North African catfish		Gill net, cast net, hook and line gear, funnel basket trap, horizontal cylinder trap	Earthworm, silkworm
10	Duk dan ดุกด้าน	North African catfish	Endangered	Gill net, cast net, hook and line gear, funnel basket trap, horizontal cylinder trap	Earthworm, silkworm
11	Duk ui ดุกอุย	Clarias macrocephalus Bighead catfish		Gill net, cast net, hook and line gear, funnel basket trap, horizontal cylinder trap	Earthworm, silkworm

195

Table 4 Ing River Ecosystem (cont.)

No.	Name	Scientific / English name	Status	Gear	Bait
12	Dut ดุก	Hypostomus plecostomus Suckerfish, suckermouth catfish		Gill net, cast net	
13	Hang daeng, khi ko หางแดง, ขี้ก้	Epalzeorhynchos frenatus	Endangered	Gill net, cast net, hook and line gear	Earthworm
14	Ian, lai เอี่ยน, ไหล	Monopterus albus Asian swamp eel		Upright basket trap, funnel basket trap	Earthworm, snail
15	Kaban hang daeng กะบาลหางแดง		Endangered	Gill net, cast net	Earthworm
16	Kaban hang khao กะบาลหางขาว		Endangered	Gill net, cast net	Earthworm
17	Kaban, chang yiap, ngae กะบาล, ช้างเหยียบ, แง่	Puntioplites proctozysron	Endangered	Gill net, cast net	Cooked sticky rice
18	Kaem song แก้มช่อง		Endangered	Gill net, cast net, hook and line gear	Earthworm
19	Kaeng pla sik แกง, ปลาซิก	Cirrhinus molitorella Mud carp	Endangered	Gill net, cast net, hook and line gear, funnel basket trap	Earthworm, crab, prawn
20	Kaet, khayaeng แกด, ขะแยง	Mystus singaringan Long fatty-finned mystus	Endangered	Gill net, cast net, hook and line gear, funnel basket trap	Earthworm, preserved fish
21	Kang ค้ง	Hemibagrus wickioides	Endangered	Gill net, cast net, bamboo tube trap, horizontal cylinder trap, hook and line gear	Fingerling, small toad
22	Kang กัง	Channa gachua Red-tailed snakehead	Endangered	Hook and line gear, funnel basket trap	Earthworm
23	Khae แข้		Endangered	Gill net, cast net, hook and line gear, bamboo tube trap	Fingerling, small toad, earthworm
24	Khao ค้าว	Wallago attu Wallago	Endangered	Gill net, hook and line gear, cast net, bamboo tube trap	Fingerling, small toad, earthworm
25	Khao na, khui ram ขาวนา, คุยราม		Endangered	Gill net, cast net	
26	Khem เข็ม	Xenentodon cancilla?	Endangered	Lift net, scoop net, fish trap	
27	Khiao kai เขียวไก่	Syncrossus helodes Banded tiger loach, tiger botia	Endangered	Gill net, cast net, fish trap, funnel basket trap	Earthworm

Table 4 Ing River Ecosystem (cont.)

30	Kot luaeng กดเหลือง	Hemibagrus filamentus	Endangered	Gill net, cast net, hook and line gear, bamboo tube trap, funnel basket trap	Earthworm, preserved fish
31	Kuk lian กุกเลียน		Endangered	Gill net, cast net, hook and line gear	Earthworm
32	Lat, lueai หลาา, เลื่อย	Mastacembelus armatus Zig-zag eel		Upright basket trap, funnel basket trap	Earthworm, snail
33	Lid, lot หลิด, หลด			Upright basket trap, funnel basket trap	Earthworm, snail
34	Lim, chon หลิม, ช่อน	Channa striata Striped snakehead, snakehead murrel	Endangered	Gill net, cast net, hook and line gear, funnel basket trap	Earthworm, fingerling, small toad
35	Mahao ม้าหาว	Raiamas guttatus Burmese trout	Endangered	Bamboo tube trap, funnel basket trap, horizontal cylinder trap, cast net, gill net	Earthworm
36	Mapaep หมะแปบ	Paralaubuca typus		Funnel basket trap, horizontal cylinder trap, cast net, gill net	Earthworm, mixed food
38	Nai ใน			Gill net, cast net, hook and line gear, bamboo tube trap	Earthworm, mixed food
39	Ngiang leo, hang hiao เงียนเล้ว, หางเหี่ยว		Endangered	Gill net, cast net, hook and line gear	Earthworm
40	Nin นิล	Oreochromis niloticus Nile tilapia		Gill net, cast net, hook and line gear	Earthworm, mixed food
41	Nuan chan หวลจันทร์	Mrigal carp		Gill net, cast net, hook and line gear, funnel basket trap	Earthworm, cooked sticky rice
42	Pak wit ปากหวิด		Endangered		
43	Phia เพี้ย	Morulius chrysophekadion Greater black shark	Endangered	Bamboo tube trap, funnel basket trap, horizontal cylinder trap, cast net, gill net	Earthworm, silkworm, snail
44	Pik daeng ปีกแดง	Barbonymus altus Red-tailed tinfoil	Endangered	Bamboo tube trap, upright basket trap	Rotten corn
45	Pok pom ปกป้อม	Systomus orphoides Red-cheek barb	Endangered		
46	Rak kluai, ha kluai รากกล้วย, ห่ากล้วย	Acantopsis spp.		Cast net, lift net, scoop net	
47	Sadet ระเด็ด	Anabas testudineus Common climbing perch		Gill net, cast net, hook and line gear, funnel basket trap	Earthworm, prawn, crab

Table 4 Ing River Ecosystem (cont.)

48	Salak สลาก	Trichogaster microlepis Moonlight gourami		Cast net, hook and line gear, funnel basket trap	Earthworm
49	Sapak สะปาก	Hypsibarbus vernayi		Gill net cast net, hook and line gear, funnel basket trap	Earthworm
50	Satup, mo thet สะตุ๊บ, หมอเทศ	Pristolepis fasciatus Striped tiger nandid		Gill net, cast net, lift net, funnel basket trap	
51	Sik สิก	Hampala macrolepidota Hampala barb		Gill net, cast net, hook and line gear, funnel basket trap	Earthworm, mixed food
52	Sio ao สิวอ้าว	Luciosoma spilopleura Apollo sharkminnow		Cast net, lift net, scoop net, hook and line gear	Earthworm, preserved fish
53	Sio bang สิวบาง	Chela caeruleostigmata Blue hachetfish, flying barb		Cast net, lift net, scoop net, hook and line gear	Earthworm, preserved fish
54	Sio khao สิวขาว	Rasbora septemtrionalis	Endangered	Cast net, lift net, scoop net, hook and line gear	Earthworm, preserved fish
55	Tong dao, tong kai ทองดาว, ทองไก่	Chitala ornata Spotted featherback	Endangered	Gill net, cast net, hook and line gear, bamboo tube trap	Earthworm, silkworm
56	Tong mueang ทองเมือง	Notopterus notopterus Grey featherback		Gill net, cast net, hook and line gear, bamboo tube trap	Earthworm, silkworm
57	Waen แว่น	Parambassis siamensis		Cast net, lift net, scoop net	
58	Wan หวาน	Kryptopterus cheveyi	Endangered	Cast net, gill net, lift net, hook and line gear	Earthworm, silkworm
59	Yi sok ยี่สก	Mrigal carp Cirrhinus cirrhosus		Gill net, cast net, hook and line gear	Earthworm, mixed food
60	Yon ยอน	Pangasius macronema	Endangered	Gill net, cast net, lift net	

198

Table 5 Ban Pak Ing—River and Inland Wetlands Ecosystem

No.	Local name	Scientific name/ Common name	Status	Fishing technique	Bait
1	Bok บอก	Henicorhynchus sp.	Endangered	Gill net, lift net	
2	Bok kled thi บอกเกล็ดถี่	Thynichthys thynnoides	Endangered	Gill net, lift net	
3	Bok laem บอกแหลม	Henicorhynchus lobatus	Endangered	Gill net, lift net	
4	Bok liam บอกเหลี่ยม	Barbichthys nitidus / Sucker barb	Endangered	Gill net, lift net	
5	Bok mon บอกมน	Henicorhynchus siammensis / Siamese mud carp	Endangered	Gill net, lift net	
6	Bok soi บอกซ้อย	Henicorhynchus spp.	Endangered	Gill net, lift net	
7	Bu ปู	Oxyeleotris marmoratus / Marble goby	Endangered	Gill net, cast net	
8	Chado ชะโด	Channa micropeltes / Giant snakehead	Endangered	Gill net, hook and line gear, hang line fishing, funnel basket trap	Fingerling
9	Chok sai ชอกทราย	Cyclocheilichthys armatus	Endangered	Gill net, cast net	
10	Dang daeng ดังแดง	Hemisilurus mekongensis	Endangered	Gill net, scoop net	
11	Dap lao ดาบลาว	Macrochirichthys macrochirus / Sword minnow	Endangered	Gill net	
12	Duk na ดุกนา	Clarias gariepinus / North African catfish	Endangered	Gill net, cast net, hook and line gear	Earthworm
13	Duk ui ดุกอุย	Clarias macrocephalus / Bighead catfish	Endangered	Gill net, cast net, hook and line gear	Earthworm
14	Dut ดุด	Hypostomus plecostomus / Suckerfish, suckermouth catfish	Endangered	Gill net,	
15	Fa mai ฟ้ามัย	Amphotistes laoensis	Endangered	Hook and line gear, funnel basket	
16	Fa ong ฟ้าออง	Amyda cartilagenea / Common Asiatic softshell	Extinct	Funnel basket trap	
17	Hang daeng หางแดง	Epalzeorhynchos frenatus / Rainbow sharkminnow	Endangered	Gill net, cast net, lift net	

199

Table 5 Ban Pak Ing—River and Inland Wetlands Ecosystem (cont.)

	lan เอียน	Monopterus albus Asian swamp eel	Endangered	Basket eel trap	Rotten crab, rotten prawn
18					
19	Ka กะ	Tor tambroides Thai mahseer	Extinct	Gill net	
20	Kaban, chang yiap, ngae กะบาล, ช้างเหยียบ, แง่	Puntioplites proctozysron	Endangered	Gill net, lift net	
21	Kae แก้	Pseudomystus siamensis Asian bumblebee catfish	Endangered	Gill net, cast net, handled scoop net	
22	Kaeng แกง	Cirrhinus molitorella Mud carp	Endangered	Gill net, cast net, lift net, pole and line fly fishing, scoop net, funnel basket trap	Preserved fish
23	Kaet แกต	Mystus atrifasciatus	Endangered	Gill net, pole and line fly fishing	Preserved fish, insect
24	Kang คัง	Hemibagrus wickioides	Endangered	Gill net, hook and line gear, hang line fishing, cast net, scoop net	Earthworm, fingerling, insect
25	Kang กั๋ง	Channa gachua Red-tailed snakehead	Endangered	Hook and line gear, cast net	Earthworm
26	Khae dam แค่ดำ	Bagarius bagarius Goonch	Endangered	Gill net, hook and line gear, hang line fishing, bamboo tube trap, funnel basket trap, scoop net	Fingerling, ant, moth, insect
27	Khae lueang แค่เหลือง	Bagarius yarrelii Goonch	Endangered	Gill net, hook and line gear, hang line fishing, bamboo tube trap, funnel basket trap, scoop net	Fingerling, ant, moth, insect
28	Khang lai ข้างลาย 1	Dangila siamensis	Endangered	Gill net, cast net	
29	Khang lai 1 ข้างลาย	Labiobarbus leptocheila	Endangered	Gill net, cast net	
30	Khao ค้าว	Wallago attu Wallago	Endangered	Gill net, hook and line gear, hang line fishing, funnel basket trap, scoop net	Fingerling, weevil
31	Khem เข็ม	Xenantodon cancilla	Endangered	Lift net, handled scoop net	
32	Khiang เคียง	Lobocheilus cf. quadrilineata	Endangered	Gill net, cast net	
33	Khiao kai เขียวไก่	Syncrossus helodes Banded tiger loach, tiger botia	Endangered	Gill net, lift net	
34	Khop bang ขบบาง	Belodontichthys truncatus	Endangered	Gill net, scoop net	

Table 5 Ban Pak Ing—River and Inland Wetlands Ecosystem (cont.)

35	Khun ขุน	Wallagonia micropogon	Extinct	Gill net, hook and line gear, hang line fishing, funnel basket trap, scoop net	Fingerling
36	Khwai kha, man mut ควายคำ, มันมุด	Gyrinocheilus spp.	Endangered	Gill net	
37	Kot dam กดคำ	Hemibagrus wickii Baung jaksa, crystal-eyed catfish	Endangered	Gill net, hook and line gear, hang line fishing, cast net, scoop net, basket trap	Earthworm, prawn, insect, weevil, moth, ant, preserved fish, earth cockroach
38	Kot khao กดขาว	Hemibagrus filamentus	Endangered	Gill net, hook and line gear, hang line fishing, cast net, scoop net, basket trap	Earthworm, prawn, insect, weevil, moth, ant, preserved fish
39	Kuk huean กุกเฮือน	Labiobarbus leptocheila	Endangered	Gill net, cast net	
40	Kwang กว่าง	Cosmochilus harmandi	Endangered	Gill net, cast net, lift net, funnel basket trap	
41	Lat หลาด	Mastacembelus armatus Zig-zag eel	Endangered	Gill net, pole and line fly fishing, bamboo tube trap	Earthworm
42	Lim หลิม	Channa striata Striped snakehead, snakehead murrel	Endangered	Hook and line gear, pole and line fly fishing, cast net	Earthworm, fingerling
43	Loem เลิม	Pangasius sanitwongsei Chao Phraya giant catfish	Extinct	Gill net, hook and line gear, pole and line fly fishing, the bottle gourd-shaped hook fishing	Cricket, fingerling
44	Lot หลด	Macrognathus semiocellatus	Endangered	Hook and line gear, box and line fishing	Earthworm
45	Man มัน	Crossocheilus reticulatus	Endangered	Gill net, cast net	
46	Man mup มันมุบ	Schistura spp.	Endangered	Lift net, hook and line gear, pole and line fly fishing	
47	Mang มั่ง	Cyclocheilichthys armatus	Endangered	Gill net, cast net	
48	Mang มาง	Barbonymus gonionotus Silver barb	Endangered	Gill net	
49	Mapaep มะแปบ	Paralaubuca typus	Endangered	Gill net, cast net, lift net, pole and line fly fishing	Preserved fish, cooked rice
50	Mapaep 1 มะแปบ 1	Paralaubuca harmandi	Endangered	Gill net, cast net, lift net, pole and line fly fishing	Preserved fish, cooked rice

Table 5 Ban Pak Ing—River and Inland Wetlands Ecosystem (cont.)

#	Local name	Scientific / common name	Status	Fishing gear	Bait
51	Mon มอน	Scaphiodonichthys acanthopterus	Endangered	Gill net, cast net	
52	Mong od โมงอด	Pangasius conchopilus	Endangered	Gill net, bottle gourd-shaped hook fishing, lift net	Fig
53	Mong yang โมงยาง	Pangasius bocourti	Endangered	Gill net, bottle gourd-shaped hook fishing, lift net	Fig
54	Nai kham ในคำ	Cyprinus rubrofuscus	Endangered	Gill net, cast net, funnel basket trap	
55	Nam fai หนามไฟ	Mystacoleucus marginatus	Endangered	Gill net, hook and line gear, pole and line fly fishing	Moth
56	Nam fai 1 หนามไฟ 1	Mystacoleucus argenteus	Endangered	Gill net, hook and line gear, pole and line fly fishing	Moth
57	Ngoen เงิน		Extinct		
58	Nin นิล	Oreochromis niloticus Nile talapia	Endangered	Gill net	
59	Nok khao นกขาว	Osteochilus schlegelii Giant sharkminnow	Endangered	Gill net, cast net	
60	Nuan jan หนวดจันทร์	Cirrhinus cirrhosus Mrigal carp	Endangered	Gill net, funnel basket trap	
61	Oen เอิน	Probarbus jullieni Jullien's golden carp	Extinct	Gill net, cast net	
62	Pak pao ปักเป้า	Monotrete turgidus Brown puffer	Endangered	Gill net, cast net	
63	Phia เพีย	Morulius chrysophykadian Greater black shark	Endangered	Gill net, cast net, lift net, scoop net, funnel basket trap	
64	Pik daeng ปีกแดง	Barbonymus altus Red-tailed tinfoil	Endangered	Gill net, cast net, hook and line gear	Cooked rice
65	Pok 1 โปก 1		Endangered	Gill net	
66	Pok 2 โปก 2		Endangered	Gill net	
67	Pok pom ปกป้อม	Systomus orphoides Red-cheek barb	Endangered	Gill net	
68	Pok pom 1 ปกป้อม 1		Endangered	Gill net	

Table 5 Ban Pak Ing—River and Inland Wetlands Ecosystem (cont.)

#	Local name	Scientific / common name	Status	Fishing technique	Bait
69	Pok yao ปกยาว		Endangered	Gill net	
70	Rak kuai รากกล้วย		Endangered	Handled scoop net, lift net	
71	Sa รก	Catlocarpio siamensis / Siamese giant carp	Extinct	Gill net	
72	Sadet สะเด็ด	Anabas testudineus / Common climbing perch	Endangered	Lift net, cast net	
73	Sai ทราย	Helicophagus leptorhynchus	Endangered	Gill net	
74	Sakang สะกาง	Puntioplites bulu	Endangered	Gill net	
75	Salat สะลาด	Trichogaster microlepis / Moonlight gourami	Endangered	Cast net, lift net	
76	Samok ซีโมก	Micronema micronema	Endangered	Gill net, hook and line gear, pole and line / fly fishing, scoop net, funnel basket trap	Fingerling
77	Sanak สนาก	Aaptosyax grypus / Giant salmon carp	Extinct	Gill net	
78	Sapak สะโปก	Hypsibarbus vernayi	Endangered	Gill net, cast net, lift net	
79	Sapak 1 สะโปก 1	Hypsibarbus malcolmi / Goldfin tinfoil barb	Endangered	Gill net, cast net, lift net	
80	Sapak 2 สะโปก 2	Hypsibarbus wetmorei	Endangered	Gill net, cast net, lift net	
81	Satup, mo thet สะตุ๊บ, หมอเทศ	Pristolepis fasciatus / Striped tiger nandid	Endangered	Gill net, cast net	
82	Sik สิก	Hampala macrolepidota / Hampala barb	Endangered	Gill net, cast net, lift net	
83	Sio ao ซีโอ้า	Luciosoma bleekeri	Endangered	Handled scoop net, gill net	
84	Sio ao 1 ซีโอ้า 1	Raiamas guttatus / Burmese trout	Endangered	Gill net	
85	Sio bang ซีบาง	Chela caeruleostigmata / Blue hachetfish, flying barb	Endangered	Handled scoop net, gill net	
86	Sio khao ซีโอ้า	Rasbora tornieri / Yellowtail rasbora	Endangered	Handled scoop net, gill net	

Table 5 Ban Pak Ing—River and Inland Wetlands Ecosystem (cont.)

	Name	Scientific / Common name	Status	Gear	Bait
87	Sueam เชือม	Ompok Krattensis Butter sheat fish	Endangered		
88	Taep แต๊บ	Trichogaster trichopterus Three spot gourami	Endangered	Gill net, cast net, hook and line gear	
89	Thapthim ทับทิม	Oreochromis niloticus niloticus Nile tilapia	Endangered	Gill net	
90	Tong ตอง	Notopterus notopterus Grey featherback	Endangered	Gill net, cast net	
91	Tong dao ตองดาว	Chitala ornate Spotted featherback	Endangered	Gill net, cast net	
92	Wa หว้า	Labeo yunnanensis	Endangered	Gill net, cast net, lift net	
93	Wa hua ngam หว้าหัวงาม หัวหงอก	Bangana behri	Extinct	Gill net, cast net, lift net	
94	Wa mon หว้ามน	Labeo dyocheilus	Endangered	Gill net, cast net, lift net	
95	Waen แว่น	Parambassis siamensis	Endangered	Cast net, handled scoop net	
96	Wa-i หว้าอี	Bangana behri	Extinct	Gill net, cast net, lift net	
97	Wan หวาน	Kryptopterus cheveyi	Endangered	Gill net, hook and line gear	Moth, insect, dragonfly
98	Yon ยอน	Pteropangsius pleurotaenia	Endangered	Gill net, hook and line gear, pole and line fly fishing	Insect, ant, earthworm, dragonfly
99	Yon lang khiao ยอนหลังเขียว	Pangasius macronema	Endangered	Gill net, hook and line gear, pole and line fly fishing	Insect, ant, earthworm, dragonfly, moth
100	Yon lang khiao 1 ยอนหลังเขียว 1	Clupisoma sinensis	Endangered	Gill net, hook and line gear, pole and line fly fishing	Insect, ant, earthworm, dragonfly, moth

Table 6 Wetland Ecosystem of the Mekong River

No.	Local name	Scientific name/ Common name	Status	Fishing technique	Bait
1	Bok บอก	Henicorhynchus sp.	Endangered	Cast net, hook and line gear, lift net	Earthworm
2	Bok kled thi บอกเกล็ดถี่	Thynichthys thynnoides	Endangered	Cast net, hook and line gear, lift net	Earthworm, crab
3	Bok laem บอกแหลม	Henicorhynchus lobatus	Endangered	Cast net, hook and line gear, lift net, bamboo tube trap, upright basket trap	Cooked sticky rice, mixed food
4	Bok liam บอกเหลี่ยม	Barbichthys nitidus Sucker barb	Endangered	Cast net, hook and line gear, lift net, bamboo tube trap, upright basket trap	Cooked sticky rice, mixed food
5	Bok mon บอกมน	Henicorhynchus siamensis Siamese mud carp	Endangered	Cast net, hook and line gear, lift net, bamboo tube trap, upright basket trap	Cooked sticky rice, mixed food
6	Bok soi บอกสร้อย	Henicorhynchus spp.	Endangered	Cast net, hook and line gear, lift net, bamboo tube trap, upright basket trap	Cooked sticky rice, mixed food
7	Bu ปู่	Oxyeleotris marmorata Marble goby	Endangered	Cast net, lift net, scoop net	Earthworm
8	Chon, lim ช่อน, หลิม	Channa striata Striped snakehead, snakehead murrel	Endangered	Cast net, funnel basket trap, lift net	Fingerling, small toad
9	Dap lao ดาบลาว	Macrochirichthys macrochirus Sward minnow	Endangered	Cast net, funnel basket trap	Earthworm, silkworm
10	Duk dan ดุกด้าน	Clarias gariepinus North African catfish	Endangered	Cast net, funnel basket trap, lift net, upright basket trap	Earthworm, snail
11	Duk ui ดุกอุย	Clarias macrocephalus Bighead catfish	Endangered	Cast net, funnel basket trap, funnel basket trap, lift net, upright basket trap	Earthworm, snail
12	Dut ดูด	Suckerfish, suckermouth catfish	Endangered	Cast net	
13	Ian, lai เอียน, ไหล	Monopterus albus Asian swamp eel	Endangered	Upright basket trap, funnel basket trap	Earthworm, preserved fish
14	Kaban, chang yiap, ngae กระเบน, ช้างเหยียบ, แง่	Puntioplites proctozysron	Endangered	Hook and line gear, cast net, bamboo tube trap, funnel basket trap, upright basket trap	Cooked sticky rice
15	Kaet, khayaeng แกด, แขยง	Mystus singaringan Long fatty-finned mystus	Endangered	Cast net, hook and line gear, funnel basket trap	Earthworm, preserved fish
16	Kang กั้ง		Endangered	Hook and line gear, cast net, bamboo tube trap	Fingerling, small toad

Table 6 Wetland Ecosystem of the Mekong River (cont.)

	Name	Species	Status	Gear	Bait
17	Kang กั้ง	Channa gachua Red-tailed snakehead	Endangered	Hook and line gear, funnel basket trap	Earthworm
18	Khae แข้, แค่		Endangered	Cast net, hook and line gear, funnel basket trap, bamboo tube trap	Fingerling, small toad
19	Khao ค้าว	Wallago attu Wallago	Endangered	Hook and line gear, cast net, hook and line gear, bamboo tube trap	Fingerling, small toad
20	Khem เข็ม		Endangered	Lift net, scoop net	
21	Khiao kai เขียวไก่	Syncrossus helodes Banded tiger loach, tiger botia	Endangered	Cast net, funnel basket trap	Earthworm
22	Kot lueang กดเหลือง	Hemibagrus filamentus	Endangered	Hook and line gear, cast net, bamboo tube trap, funnel basket trap	Earthworm, preserved fish
23	Lat, lueai หลาด, เลือย	Mastacembelus armatus Zig-zag eel	Endangered	Upright basket trap, funnel basket trap, hook and line gear	Silkworm
24	Lot, lit หลด, หลิด	Macrognathus semiocellatus	Endangered	Upright basket trap, funnel basket trap, hook and line gear	Silkworm
25	Mahao ม้าหาว, หะหาว	Raiamas guttatus Burmese trout	Endangered	Cast net	
26	Mapaep มะแปบ	Paralaubuca typus	Endangered	Cast net, lift net	
27	Nai ไน	Cyprinus rubrofuscus	Endangered	Cast net, hook and line gear, lift net	Earthworm, crab
28	Nam pi น้ำปี้		Endangered	Cast net	
29	Nin นิล	Oreochromis niloticus Nile tilapia	Endangered	Cast net, hook and line gear, lift net	Earthworm
30	Pak liam ปากเลียม		Endangered	Cast net, hook and line gear	Earthworm
31	Pak wit ปากวิด, ปากวิค		Endangered	Cast net, hook and line gear	Earthworm
32	Phia เพี้ย	Morulius chrysophekadion Greater black shark	Endangered	Cast net, lift net, bamboo tube trap, funnel basket trap	Earthworm, silkworm
33	Pik daeng ปีกแดง	Barbonymus altus Red-tailed tinfoil	Endangered	Cast net, hook and line gear, lift net	Nod leaf
34	Pok pom ปกป้อม	Systomus orphoides Red-cheek barb	Endangered	Cast net, hook and line gear, lift net	Cooked sticky rice, mixed food

Table 6 Wetland Ecosystem of the Mekong River (cont.)

35	Rak kluai รากกล้วย	Acantopsis spp.	Endangered	Cast net, scoop net	
36	Sadet สะเด็ด	Anabas testudineus Common climbing perch	Endangered	Cast net, scoop net, hook and line gear	Earthworm, silkworm snail, crab
37	Salak สะลาก	Trichogaster microlepis Midnight gourami	Endangered	Cast net, scoop net	Earthworm, snail, crab
38	Sapak สะปาก	Hypsibarbus vernayi	Endangered	Cast net, hook and line gear	Earthworm, silkworm
39	Satup, mo thet สะตุ้บ, หมอเทศ	Pristolepis fasciatus Striped tiger nandid	Endangered	Cast net, scoop net, hook and line gear	Earthworm, silkworm, snail, crab
40	Sik สิก, ชิก	Hampala macrolepidota Hampala barb	Endangered	Cast net, scoop net, hook and line gear	Earthworm, snail, crab
41	Sio ao สิวเอ้า	Luciosoma spilopleura Apollo sharkminnow	Endangered	Cast net, lift net, scoop net	Earthworm, preserved fish
42	Sio bang สิวบาง	Chela caeruleostigmata Blue hachetfish, flying barb	Endangered	Cast net, lift net, scoop net	Earthworm, preserved fish
43	Sio khao สิวข้าว, สิวหิ้งกา	Rasbora septemtrionalis	Endangered	Cast net, lift net, scoop net	Earthworm, preserved fish
44	Tong dao, tong kai ตองดาว, ตองกาย	Chitala ornate Spotted featherback	Endangered	Cast net, funnel basket trap, horizontal cylinder trap	Earthworm, silkworm
45	Tong mueang ตองเมือง	Notopterus notopterus Grey featherback	Endangered	Cast net, funnel basket trap, horizontal cylinder trap	Earthworm, silkworm
46	Waen kaeo แว่นแก้ว	Parambassis siamensis	Endangered	Cast net, lift net	
47	Wan วาน	Kryptopterus cheveyi	Endangered	Cast net, lift net	Earthworm, silkworm
48	Yi sok, nuan chan ยี่สก, นวลจันทร์	Cirrhinus cirrhosus Mrigal carp	Endangered	Cast net, hook and line gear	
49	Yon ยอน	Pangasius macronema	Endangered	Cast net, lift net	

References

Allan, J. D., R. Abell, Z. Hogan, C. Revenga, and B. W. Taylor. 2005. "Overfishing of Inland Waters." *Bioscience* 55 (12).

Asian Development Bank. 2000. The Greater Mekong Subregion Economic Cooperation Program. GMS Assistance Plan (2001–2003), December 2000.

Agrawal, A. 1995. "Indigenous and Scientific Knowledge: Some Critical Comments." *Indigenous Knowledge and Development Monitor* 3 (3): 1–8.

Anan Ganjanapan. 1998. "The Politics of Conservation and the Complexity of Local Control of Forest in the Northern Thai Highlands." *Mountain Research and Development* 18 (1): 71–82.

Appadurai, A. 2001. "Grassroots Globalization and the Research Imagination." In *Globalization,* edited by A. Appadurai. Durham: Duke University Press.

———. 2006. "Foreword". In *Transnational Civil Society: An Introduction*, edited by S. Batliwala and L. D. Brown. Bloomfield, CT: Kumarian Press.

Baran, E. and I. G. Baird. 2003. "Approaches and Tools for Sustainable Management of Fish Resources in the Mekong River Basin." In *Biodiversity Management and Sustainable Development: Lancang-Mekong River in the New Millennium,* edited by M. Cao, K. Woods, H. Hu, and L. Li. Kunming: China Forestry Publishing House.

Barnet, R. and J. Cavanagh. 1994. *Global Dreams: Imperial Corporations and the New World Order.* New York: Simon and Schuster.

Batliwala, S. and L. D. Brown, eds. 2006. *Transnational Civil Society: An Introduction.* Bloomfield, CT: Kumarian Press.

Berkes, F. 2002. "Cross-Scale Institutional Linkages: Perspectives From the Bottom Up." In *The Drama of the Commons*, edited by E. Ostrom et al. Washington DC: National Academy Press.

Blake, D. J. H. 2001. "The Status, Threats to and Potential of Flood Zone Agriculture in the Lower Mekong Basin, with Reference to a Case Study on Two Major Lowland Rivers in Northeast Thailand." M.Sc. dissertation, Imperial College at Wye, Unversity of London.

————. 2003. "Riverbank Vegetable Cropping in the Lower Mekong Basin: A Highly Sustainable Farming System or an Anachronism Doomed to Oblivion?" In *Biodiversity Management and Sustainable Devleopment: Lancang-Mekong River in the New Millennium*, edited by M. Cao, K. Woods, H. Hu and L. Li. Kunming: China Forestry Publishing House.

————. 2004. "Riverbank Vegetable Cropping in the Lower Mekong Basin: A Sustainable Farming System Doomed to Oblivion?" *Watershed* 10(1): 62–72.

Borrini-Feyerabend, G. 2000. *Co-management of Natural Resources: Organising, Negotiating and Learning by Doing.* Yaoundé: International Union for the Conservation of Nature (IUCN).

Burgerman, S. 2001. *Moral Victories: How Activists Provoke Multilateral Action.* Ithaca, NY: Cornell University Press.

Bush, S. 2003. "'Give a Man a Fish': Contextualising Living Aquatic Resources Development in the Lower Mekong Basin." Working Paper No. 8, Australian Mekong Resource Centre, University of Sydney.

Campbell, I. 2003. "Invertebrates, Biodiversity and the Upper Lancang-Mekong Navigation Project." In *Biodiversity Management and Sustainable Development: Lancang-Mekong River in the New Millennium*, edited by M. Cao, K. Woods, H. Hu, and L. Li. Kunming: China Forestry Publishing House.

Chavalit Vidthayanon. 2004. *Handbook of Freshwater Fish* (in Thai). Bangkok: Sarakhadi.

————. 2008. *Field Guide to Fishes of the Mekong Delta.* Vientiane: Mekong River Commission.

Cheong, G. 1998. "Resource Management in the Lao Mekong Basin." Working Paper No. 73, Asia Research Centre, Murdoch University.

Claridge, G. F., compiler. 1996. "An Inventory of Wetlands of the Lao PDR." Bangkok: IUCN.

Coates, D. 2001. "Biodiversity and Fisheries Management Opportunities in the Mekong River Basin." Paper presented at the international workshop "Blue Millennium: Managing Global Fisheries for Biodiversity," World Fisheries Trust, Victoria, Canada.

Coates D. et al. 2003. "Biodiversity and Fisheries in the Lower Mekong Basin." *Mekong Development Series* No. 2. Phnom Penh: Mekong River Commission.

Cohen, P. T. 1981. "The Politics of Economic Development in Northern Thailand, 1967–1978." Ph.D. dissertation, University of London.

———. 1984. "Opium and the Karen: A Study of Indebtedness in Northern Thailand." *Journal of Southeast Asian Studies 15*(1): 150–165.

Comaroff, J. L. and J. Comaroff, eds. 1999. *Civil Society and the Political Imagination in Africa*. Chicago: University of Chicago Press.

Conklin, H. 1954. "The Relation of Hanunuo Culture to the Plant World." Ph.D. dissertation. Yale University.

———. 1961. "The Study of Shifting Cultivation. *Current Anthropology* 2: 27–61.

Delang, C. O. 2002. "Deforestation in Northern Thailand: The Result of Hmong Farming Practices or Thai Development Strategies?" *Society & Natural Resources* 15(6): 483–501.

Department of Water Resources. 2004. *Report on Water Flow of the Mekong River*. Bangkok: Department of Water Resources.

Dearden P. 1995. "Biocultural Diversity and Development in Northern Thailand." *Applied Geography* 15: 325–340.

Dien, N. T. 2002. "Dynamism of Local Ecological Knowledge: A Case Study of a Muong Community in Northern Vietnam." M.A. Thesis, Regional Centre for Soial Science and Sustainable Development (RCSD), Chiang Mai University.

Dirksen H. 1997. "Solving Problems of Opium Production in Thailand." In *Development or Domestication: Indigenous Peoples of Southeast Asia*, edited by D. McCaskill and Kampe K. Chiang Mai: Silkworm Books.

Donnelly, N. D. 1994. *Changing Lives of Refugee Hmong Women*. Seattle: University of Washington Press.

Dudgeon, D. 2003. "What Constrains the Conservation of Riverine Biodiversity in Asia?" In *Biodiversity Management and Sustainable Devleopment: Lancang-Mekong River in the New Millennium*, edited by M. Cao, K. Woods, H. Hu, and L. Li. Kunming: China Forestry Publishing House.

The Ecologist. 1992. *Whose Common Future? Reclaiming the Commons*. Dorset: The Ecologist.

Ekins, P. 1990. "Forward". In *For the Common Good: Redirecting the Economy Toward Community, the Environment, and a Sustainable Future*, edited by H. E. Daly and J. B. Cobb Jr. London: Green Print.

Evangelista, M. 1999. *Unarmed Forces: The Transnational Movement to End the Cold War*. Ithaca, NY: Cornell University Press.

Evans, G. 1988. *Agrarian Change in Communist Laos*. Singapore: Institute of Southeast Asian Studies.

————. 1990. *Lao Peasants under Socialism*. New Haven: Yale University Press.

————. 1995. *Lao Peasants under Socialism and Post-Socialism*. Chiang Mai: Silkworm Books.

FishBase Consortium. http://fish.mongabay.com/data/ecosystems/Mekong%20 River htm; http://www.fishbase.org/. (A reference of fish names).

Florini, A., ed. 1999. *The Third Forces: The Rises of Transnational Civil Society*. Tokyo and Washington: Japan Center for International Change and Carnegie Endowment for International Peace.

Geddes, W. R. 1976. *Migrants of the Mountains: The Cultural Ecology of the Blue Miao (Hmong Njua) of Thailand*. Oxford: Oxford University Press.

Gragson, T. L. and B. G. Blount, eds. 1999. *Ethnoecology: Knowledge, Resources, and Rights*. Athens: University of Georgia Press.

Grandstaff, T. B. 1980. *Shifting Cultivation in Northern Thailand: Possibilities for Development*. Tokyo: United Nations University.

Guttal, S. and B. Shoemaker. 2004. "Manipulating Consent: The World Bank and Public Consultation in the Nam Theun 2 Hydroelectric Project." *Watershed* 10(1): 18–29.

Halpern, J. M. 1958. *Aspects of Village Life and Cultural Change in Laos*. New York: Council on Economic and Cultural Affairs.

Hartmann, W. et al., 2004. "People and Fisheries Management". In *Proceedings of the Second International Symposium on the Management of Large Rivers for Fisheries*, vol. 1, edited by R. L. Welcomme and T. Petr. Bangkok: Food and Agricultural Organization of the United Nations, Regional Office for Asia and the Pacific.

Hill, M. T and S. A. Hill. 1994. *Fisheries Ecology and Hydropower in the Mekong River: An Evaluation of Run-of-the-River Projects*. Ensuing Technical Paper for AusAID Mekong Basin Natural Resources Management Project. Vientiane: Mekong Secretariat.

Hirsch, P. and G. Choeng. 1996. *Natural Resource Management in the Mekong River Basin: Perspectives for Australian Development Cooperation*. Final Overview Report to AusAID.

Hoffman, T. 1997. "Moving Beyond Dualism: A Dialogue with Western European and American Indian Vews of Spirituality, Nature and Science." *Social Science Journal* 34(4): 447–460.

Hsieh, S. 1989. "Ethnic-Political Adaptation and Ethnic Change of the Sipsong Panna Dai: An Ethnohistorical Analysis." Ph.D. Dissertation in Anthropology. Seattle: University of Washington.

International Rivers Network. 1999. *Power Struggle: The Impacts of Hydro-Development in Laos.*

Jensen, J. G. 1996. "1,000,000 Tons of Fish from the Mekong?" *Mekong Fish Catch and Culture* 2 (1).

———. 2001. "Traditional Fish Products: The Milk of Southeast-Asia". *Mekong Fish Catch and Culture* 6 (4).

Jiazheng, P. and Z. Jinsheng. 1993. "Hydropower Development in China." *Water Power and Dam Construction*, February, 12–13.

Khagram, S., J. V. Riker and K. Sikkink, eds. 2002. *Restructuring World Politics: Transnational Social Movements, Networks, and Norms.* Minneapolis: University of Minnesota Press.

Kham Lee. 2003. "Social Challenges for Lao PDR." In 2003. *Social Challenges for the Mekong Region*, edited by Mingsarn Kaosa-ard and J. Dore. Chiang Mai: Social Research Institute, Chiang Mai University.

Lestrelin, G., M. Giordano, and Bounmy Keohavong. 2005. "When 'Conservation' Leads to Land Degradation: Lessons from Ban Lak Sip, Laos." Research Report 91. Colombo: International Water Management Institute.

Lohman, L. 1991. "Peasants, Plantations and Pulp: The Politics of Eucalyptus in Thailand." *Bulletin of Concerned Asian Scholars* 23(4): 3–17.

Makim, A. 2002. "The Changing Face of Mekong Resource Politics in the Post-Cold War Era: Renogotiating Arrangements for Water Resource Management in the Lower Mekong River Basin (1991–1995)." Sydney: Australian Mekong Resource Center, Working Paper No. 6.

Mattson, N. S. et al. 2003. "The Role of Giant Fish Species in Managing the Mekong Ecosystem." In *Biodiversity Management and Sustainable Devleopment: Lancang-Mekong River in the New Millennium*, edited by M. Cao, K. Woods, H. Hu, and L. Li. Kunming: China Forestry Publishing House.

Merchant, C. 1992. *Radical Ecology: The Search for a Livable World.* New York: Routledge.

Mekong Secretariat. 1992. *Fisheries in the Lower Mekong Basin. Main Report.* Bangkok: Interim Committee for Coordination of Investigations of the Lower Mekong Basin.

———. 1994. "Fisheries Ecology and Hydropower in the Mekong River: An Evaluation of Run-of-the-River Projects." Bangkok: Mekong Secretariat.

Mekong River Commission. 2005. "Deep Pools as Dry Season Habitats in the Mekong River Basin." Mekong Fisheries Management Recommendation No. 3. Vientiane: Technical Advisory Body for Fisheries Management (TAB).

Miller, F. and P. Hirsch. 2003. "Civil Society and Internationalized River Basin Management." Working Paper No. 7. Australian Mekong Resource Center, Sydney University.

Mingsarn Kaosa-ard. 2003. "Poverty and Globalisation." In *Social Challenges for the Mekong Region*, edited by Mingsarn Kaosa-ard and J. Dore. Chiang Mai: Social Research Institute, Chiang Mai University.

Mingsarn Kaosa-ard and J. Dore, eds. 2003. *Social Challenges for the Mekong Region*. Chiang Mai: Social Research Institute, Chiang Mai University.

Naiyana Vichitporn. 2001. "The Transformation of Gender Roles in Resource Management of a Karen Community in Northern Thailand." M.A. thesis, Research Centre for Social Science and Sustainable Development, Chiang Mai University.

Nazarea, V. D. ed. 1999. *Ethnoecology: Situated Knowledge/Located Lives.* Tucson: University of Arizona Press.

Nygren, A. 1999. "Local Knowledge in the Environment-Development Discourse." *Critique of Anthropology* 19(3): 267–288.

Olivier Evrard and Yves Goudineau. 2004. "Planned Resettlement, Unexpected Migrations and Cultural Trauma in Laos." *Development and Change* 35(5): 937–962.

Onideth Souksavat, et al. 2000. "An Investigation into the Life-cycle, Biology and Potential used in Aquaculture of Selected Indigenous Freshwater Prawns in Northern Mekong Tributaries of the Lao PDR." Vientiane: Living Aquatic Resource Center.

Osborn, M. 2004. "River at Risk: The Mekong and the Water Politics of China and Southeast Asia." Lowy Institute Paper 02, Lowy Institute for International Policy, Sydney.

———. 2006. "The Paramount Power: China and the Countries of Southeast Asia. Lowy Institute Paper 11, Lowy Institute for International Policy, Sydney.

———. 2007. "The Water Politics of China and Southeast Asia II: Rivers, Dams, Cargo Boats and the Environment." Lowy Institute Perspectives Paper, Lowy Institute for International Policy, Sydney.

Ostrom, E. et al. eds. 2002. *The Drama of the Commons*. Washington DC: National Academy Press.

Phetsavanh Sayboualavan. 2004a. The Forgotten Victims of the Nam Leuk Dam in Laos: Summary of Fact-Finding Trip to Affected Villages. Unpublished.

————. 2004b. Hydroelectric Dams and the Forgotten People of the Boloven Plateau. Unpublished.

Piyaporn Wongruang, 2003. "Mekong Fishermen Left High and Dry". In *Invisible Borders: Reportage from Our Mekong.* Bangkok: IPS Asia-Pacific Regional Center.

Poffenberger, M. and R. D. Stone, 1996 "Hidden Faces in the Forest: A Twenty-First Century Challenge for Tropical Asia." *SAIS Review* 16(1): 203–219.

Poulsen, A. F. and J. Valbo-Jorgensen, eds., 2000. "Fish Migration and Spawning Habits in the Mekong Mainstream: A Survey Using Local Knowledge." AMFC Technical Report. Phnom Penh: Mekong River Commission. *Watershed* 10(1): 52–59.

Poulsen, A. F. et al. 2002. *Deep Pools as Dry Season Fish Habitats in the Mekong Basin.* Technical Paper No. 4. Vientiane: Mekong River Commission.

Poulsen, A. F. and Sinthavong Viravong. 2003. "Fish Migrations and the Maintenance of Biodiversity in the Mekong River Basin." In *Biodiversity Management and Sustainable Devleopment: Lancang-Mekong River in the New Millennium,* edited by M. Cao, K. Woods, H. Hu, and L. Li. Kunming: China Forestry Publishing House.

Prachoom Chomchai. 1992. "Planning the Development of the Mekong River Basin." *Water Power and Dam Construction,* October, 34–38.

Price, R. 2003. "Transnational Civil Society and Advocacy in World Politics." *World Politics* 55(4): 579–606.

Phrek Gypmantasiri. 1993. "Sustainable Agricultural Practices on Highland of Northern Thailand." *Agricultural Technical Report* No. 34, Multiple Cropping Center, Faculty of Agriculture, Chiang Mai University.

Restorp, U. 2000. "Improved Fallow Systems in the Luang Prabang Area, Lao PDR." Sweden: Earth Sciences Centre, Goteborg University.

Roberts, T. R. 1993. "Artisanal Fisheries and Fish Ecology below the Great Waterfalls of the Mekong River in Southern Lao." *Natural History Bulletin of the Siam Society* 41: 31–62.

Roberts, T. R. and I. G. Baird. 1995. "Traditional Fisheries and Fish Ecology on the Mekong River in Southern Laos." *Natural History Bulletin of the Siam Society* 43: 219–262.

Samata, R. 2003 "Agricultural Transformation and Highlander Choice: A Case Study of a Pwo Karen Community in Northwestern Thailand." M.A. Thesis in Sustainable Development, RCSD, Chiang Mai University.

Searin (Southeast Asia Rivers Network). 2002. *Mae Mun: The Return of the Fisherfolk.* (In Thai). Bangkok: Searin–Thailand,

Shoemaker, B., I. G. Baird and M. Baird. 2001. *The People and Their River: A Survey of River-Based Livelihoods in the Xe Bang Fai River Basin in Central Lao PDR.* Vientiane.

Sheldon, A. E. 1988. Conservation of Stream Fishes: Patterns of Diversity, Rarity, and Risk. *Conservation Biology* 2: 149–156.

Sianouvong Savathvong. 2000. "Land Use in the Highland Areas of Lao PDR: A Case Study of Huai Khang Village, Xieng Ngeun District, Luang-Prabang Province." M.A. Thesis, RCSD, Chiang Mai University.

Sibtain, S. N. 2003. *About a Village: A Field Study of Ban Na Duang, Vang Vieng District, Vientiane Province, Laos.* Vientiane: Department of Architecture, National University of Laos.

Sokheng, C., K. Chea and J. Valbo-Jorgensen, eds., 2000. "Lateral Fish Movements Between Tonle Sap River and its Flood Plain." In *Contributions to 3rd Technical Symposium on Mekong Fisheries.* Phnom Penh: Mekong River Commission.

Symonds, P. V. 2004. *Calling in the Soul: Gender and the Cycle of Life in a Hmong Village.* Seattle: University of Washington Press.

Tapp, N. 1989. *Soverignty and Rebellion: The White Hmong of Northern Thailand.* Oxford: Oxford University Press.

Thai Baan Research. 2006. *Local Knowledge of Mekong's Fish Varieties, The Mekong River* (in Thai). Chiang Rai: Thai Baan Research Team, Chiang Khong–Wiang Kaen.

Trankell, I. B. 1993. *On the Road in Laos: An Anthropological Study of Road Construction and Rural Communities.* Uppsala Research Reports in Cultural Anthropology, No. 12, Uppsala University.

Tyler, S. R. 2006. *Co-management of Natural Resources: Local Learning for Poverty Reduction.* Ottawa: International Development Research Centre.

Visser, T. and A. F. Poulsen. 2003. 'Biodiversity and the Mekong Fish Database." In *Biodiversity Management and Sustainable Development: Lancang-Mekong River in the New Millennium,* edited by M. Cao, K. Woods, H. Hu, and L. Li. Kunming: China Forestry Publishing House.

Walker, A. R. 1992. *The Highland Heritage: Collected Essays on Upland Northern Thailand.* Singapore: Suvarnabhumi Books.

Waranoot Tungittiplakorn. 1998. "Highland Cash Crop Development and Biodiversity Conservation: The Hmong in Northern Thailand." Ph.D. dissertation, Department of Geography, University of Victoria.

Waranoot Tungittiplakorn and P. Dearden, 2002. "Biodiversity Conservation and Cash Crop Development in Northern Thailand." *Biodiversity and Conservation* 11: 2007–2025.

Warner, K. 1991. *Shifting Cultivators: Local Technical Knowledge and Natural Resource Management in the Humid Tropics.* Rome: FAO.

Yos Santasombat. 1996. *Tha Kwien: Bod Wikkhroa Buang Ton Wa Duay Karn Prab Tua Khong Chumchon Chaona Thai Tham Klang Karn Pid Lawm Khong Wattanatham Utsahakham* (Tha Kwien: A Preliminary Analysis of the Adaptive Responses of a Peasant Community to Enclosure and Industrialism). Bangkok: Khob Fai.

———. 2001. *Lak Chang: Reconstruction of Tai Identity in Daikong.* Canberra: Pandanus Books, The Australian National University.

———. 2003a. *Biodiversity, Local Knowledge and Sustainable Development.* Chiang Mai: RCSD, Chiang Mai University.

———. 2003b. "Customary Rights, Ethnicity and the Politics of Location." *Thailand Human Rights Journal* (1): 121–136.

———. 2008. *Flexible Peasants: Reconceptualizing the Third World's Rural Types.* Chiang Mai: RCSD, Chiang Mai University.

Index